OUT *of*
CHAOS

PRAISE FOR

Out of Chaos

Chaos—both the inconvenience of missing a meeting and the disruption of a global pandemic—affects us every day. My friend Jessica LaGrone acknowledges how chaos, both big and small, can cause us to question even the most basic things in life, affecting our internal and external worlds and our relationships. But instead of offering a five-part plan on how to tackle chaos or eliminate it from our lives, Jessica's words help us look at chaos in a new light—not as something to be avoided at all costs, but as an opportunity for creating something new when everything we know falls apart. If your normal routines have been thrown off these last few years, you've experienced loss, or you're simply searching for a way to embrace all of life's little disruptions, pick up *Out of Chaos*.

ADAM WEBER, lead pastor of Embrace Church, author of *Love Has a Name*, and host of *The Conversation* podcast

Who hasn't said, "That's not the way I thought this would go?" in the last few years? We all have, which means we all need this book. Jessica LaGrone's calm style of masterful story-telling helps us think past the question and beyond our own chaos, disappointment, trauma, and discouragement toward the ways God so beautifully redeems even our worst moments. You will love meeting Jessica's friends and fellow travelers and be grateful for the lessons in hope to be found on every page. This is the book we all need as we emerge from a season of extraordinary chaos.

CAROLYN MOORE, pastor of Mosaic Church and author of *When Women Lead*

We are living through one of the most challenging and chaotic times in modern history. It is a strange world, where things like pandemics and protests seem to be the new norm. One thing is for certain—we live in a different world than before, and things may never return to the way they were. We cannot hope to make sense of our new world by using old maps. Jessica LaGrone has provided us with a new GPS to navigate the realities of the chaotic world. This is essential reading for anyone looking for hope in hard times. Read it, and you will find your faith renewed and your hope restored.

WINFIELD BEVINS, author of *Liturgical Mission*

There is a promise in Scripture that God works all things together for good for those who love him and are called according to his purpose. Jessica LaGrone is certainly one of those gifted and faithful persons who believes this with all her heart. Indeed, she manifests this again and again in her excellent preaching and teaching as our seminary chaplain. But still, what does one do when the chaos of a pandemic or career or family crisis unexpectedly takes over one's life? Here, in her usual creative and readable style, Jessica offers guidance about how to deal with chaos. It turns out that God can use chaos to create a brighter future for all of us who are his children. I highly recommend this book.

BEN WITHERINGTON III, Amos professor
of New Testament for doctoral studies,
Asbury Theological Seminary

In the past two years, *chaos* has become one of the most repeated words in our culture as a description of current life personally, corporately, institutionally, and globally—generally used in a hopeless tone. Jessica LaGrone has taken this word and turned it upside down. Chaos is not denied, nor is this a "positive thinking solves all the problems" book. Chaos is explored through the lens of Scripture, daily life, history and compelling personal stories. As I read this book, I had moments of surprise tears in my eyes as the words resonated with my soul. These powerful words illustrate the book's richness: "Chaos existed from the very beginning. But the chaos doesn't rule. Instead, it is ruled. It doesn't remain as it is, nor does it disappear, but it is changed." This is a significant book for these days.

JO ANNE LYON, general superintendent emerita, the Wesleyan Church

What do panic attacks, miscarriages, Alzheimer's disease, and pandemics have in common? They are among the chaotic materials Jessica LaGrone weaves together to bring hope from despair and purpose from pain. Written with a poet's flair and pastor's insight, LaGrone's new book doesn't just help us make sense of our world; it helps us make sense of our lives as well.

TALBOT DAVIS, pastor of Good Shepherd Church and author of *Simplify the Message, Multiply the Impact*

Chaos and order. Polar opposites in my mind, but Jessica LaGrone paints a more complex and beautiful picture. Even as our Creator God brings chaos into order, he also inhabits the boundary spaces between the two and uses messy chaos in the creative process of growth in our lives. As an artist or a chef or a writer knows, something formless and empty can become lovely and full. So it is with the One who orders all of life. This book is an intimate and profound exploration of God at work in these chaotic times.

BISHOP LINDA ALLEN, bishop, the Free Methodist Church

OUT *of* CHAOS

How God Makes New Things
from the Broken Pieces of Life

Jessica LaGrone

ZONDERVAN REFLECTIVE

Out of Chaos
Copyright © 2022 by Jessica LaGrone

Requests for information should be addressed to:
Zondervan, *3900 Sparks Dr. SE, Grand Rapids, Michigan 49546*

Seedbed Publishing, *415 Bridge Street, Franklin, Tennessee 37064*

Zondervan titles may be purchased in bulk for educational, business, fundraising, or sales promotional use. For information, please email SpecialMarkets@Zondervan.com.

ISBN 978-0-310-11946-3 (audio)

Library of Congress Cataloging-in-Publication Data

Names: LaGrone, Jessica, author.
Title: Out of chaos : how God makes new things from the broken pieces of life / Jessica LaGrone.
Description: Grand Rapids : Zondervan, 2022.
Identifiers: LCCN 2021050847 (print) | LCCN 2021050848 (ebook) | ISBN 9780310119449 (paperback) | ISBN 9780310119456 (ebook)
Subjects: LCSH: Suffering—Religious aspects—Christianity. | Pain—Religious aspects—Christianity. | Christian life.
Classification: LCC BV4909 .L254 2022 (print) | LCC BV4909 (ebook) | DDC 248.8/6—dc23/eng/20220120
LC record available at https://lccn.loc.gov/2021050847
LC ebook record available at https://lccn.loc.gov/2021050848

Cover design: Brock Book Design Co., Charles Brock
Cover photo: © Transfuchsian / Adobe Stock
Interior design: Kait Lamphere

Printed in the United States of America

22 23 24 25 26 27 28 29 30 31 32 /TRM/ 13 12 11 10 9 8 7 6 5 4 3 2 1

To Drew and Kate—
who are God's "good things running wild"
in my home and in my heart.
I love you always.

CONTENTS

FOREWORD

I'm a phenomenal listener. This may be the first time you've heard someone boast about that, but I really am. Those closest to me would say that when they're walking through something difficult, I'm one of the first people they turn to for a listening ear. I wish I was as handy at fixing things as I am at listening to others. But I'm not. For that matter, I'm not good at much else *besides* listening—I've just always excelled at attuning to the words and feelings of others. Sometimes I'm a little *too* good at attuning to the emotional needs of others.

There's a dark side to many of our gifts. My family of origin was an environment of seasonal peace—ups and downs and mostly a world of chaos. Swirling about me during my most formative years were addictions, alcoholism, divorce, loneliness, isolation, and family disruption and disorder. My parents did their darnedest to handle these challenges with care—but fixed in my memory of those developmental years is the constancy of chaos.

These experiences of chaos became a womb for the

development of my listening skills. Living through the mutual pain that my mother and father endured as they waded through their divorce to each other, I learned, as an only child who wanted to bring some sense of peace to the family, how to attune to *their* emotional needs. By the time I was ten, I had a graduate degree in listening. Sadly, the development of these skills thrust me onto the stage of adulthood far too quickly. I became an emotional caregiver to my parents as they grieved the loss of their identity and marriage to each other. Not that they demanded it of me. But it changed me all the same. Instead of getting to be a child, I became a counselor to grieving adults—all before I experienced puberty.

So, yes, I'm a world-class listener. But that gift has come with some scars—as many of our gifts do. In recent years I've done some rudimentary emotional archaeology in the safe care of spiritual direction, and this has helped me see why I'm such a good listener who innately knows how to attune to others. I listen as well as I do because the pain of my childhood forced me to learn this skill early in life. And in my worst moments, I tend to overlisten as a means of deflecting—to avoid fully engaging in a conversation where I may need to reveal my inner self.

There's an odd principle at play here—namely, that many of our greatest gifts are forged in the fires of pain and difficulty. This is often God's way of making us who we are. He takes the raw materials of difficulty and puts together a miracle. For the ancient witness of Scripture, this principle is placed on the lips of Joseph speaking to his brothers: "You intended to harm me, but God intended it for good" (Genesis 50:20). Indeed, in the Christian story this is one of most important theological realities: chaos is the palette from which God makes the world. And it is out of our own chaos that God forms and makes us into the people we are becoming.

The modern Christian doesn't have much of an imagination to draw from when it comes to the difficulties of reality. In all my years of pastoral work, I have often seen people run away in the chaos of life, deconstructing their faith and abandoning their love for God. *Why would God allow the suffering of a child? Why would God allow me to walk through a divorce? Why didn't God stop the trauma that was done to me as a child?* Our own loss becomes the reason we abandon the God who made us. Too often, we refuse to see chaos and difficulty as realms in which God can do any good work. And so in great disappointment, our faith shrinks or is abandoned altogether. Rather than running to God *in* our chaos, we abandon him once again.

Behind this shallow imagination lurks a false expectation about the way we thought the world would work—perfectionist expectations that falsely believe the world would have been better off stripped of the chaos. But that isn't how God works. God never created a perfect world—a static existence free from change or even the possibility of sin and evil. God created a *good* world, one over which God declares time and time again, "*Tov, tov, tov.*" Good, good, good indeed. Perfect? No! A good world is still a world that contains chaos.

The gift that Jessica LaGrone has offered the church here has been forged in the fires of great pain and tribulation.

But she has brought a gift for us out of the fire. The following pages offer an invitation to a different way—the way of Jesus. For Jesus does not call us *out of* a world of chaos. Rather, in Jesus, God enters our world of chaos to meet us there. And it is into the chaos of our difficulties, our pain, our responsibility, our failure, and our day-to-day challenges that God calls us. This is what the incarnation is.

> *A. J. Swoboda, PhD,*
> Advent 2021

INTRODUCTION

My husband, Jim, and I once went on a road trip, leaving his parents behind to house-sit for us in our absence. About halfway into our five-hour drive out of state, the power steering on his car began to stiffen up a bit. The longer we drove, the tougher the car was to turn, and by the time we pulled into the busy city streets around our hotel, Jim was straining, arm over arm, to turn the car around the tight city blocks as if turning the wheel of an enormous ship.

After locating a repair shop in an unfamiliar city and paying dearly for repairs, Jim called home to check in, only to be told our dishwasher wasn't working. A visit from the appliance repairman revealed that it was completely dead. A replacement was ordered but found to be weeks away from delivery. With the car repaired, we returned home and opened our refrigerator to find balmy, tepid conditions—certainly not the chill you'd like for your salmon or mayonnaise. The (now very familiar) repairman returned with good and bad news. This appliance was resurrectable with a simple part, but it might be a month before it could be delivered and installed. We began to pray that the adage about bad things happening in threes would cap our troubles.

It was amazing to me just how much of our smooth daily existence could be thrown into chaos with the breakdown of a few machines. I'd love to tell you quaint stories of how washing and drying dishes together by hand made us grow closer as a couple, but *Little House on the Prairie* we were not. Reality looked a bit more like one of us yelling, "Don't let all the cold air out!" across the house when the other one opened the series of coolers lining our dining room that held milk and basic necessities in rapidly melting ice water. There were times when the breakdown of our modern conveniences made me feel close to breakdown myself. Under financial strain and out of our usually predictable routine, we found ourselves easily irritated, arguing over small things that normally wouldn't have been a bother. Somehow the disturbance from the outside had crept under our skin, making our internal landscapes as chaotic as the outside. Things can fall apart. Sometimes we do too.

An Unwelcome Visitor

Chaos is no stranger in most of our lives. If we're paying attention, we know life can deteriorate into a hot mess on any given day. There's a steady daily drip of what we might call "everyday chaos": the bedlam of just getting everyone out the door in the morning, the rush to meet a work deadline, navigating the tangle of tense family relationships—some of them with a lifetime or more of complicated backstories. Anyone who has ever tried to organize a group presentation or a family photo shoot or even their own thoughts knows chaos's calling card—the unraveling of our plans followed by a headshaking, disorienting realization: *That's not the way I hoped this would go.*

A friend once told me she spent the workweek at her desk dreaming of the weekend ahead as a peaceful oasis of doing nothing. But by Saturday, the list of errands and household to-dos that had accumulated during the week filled her weekend to the edges, and she found herself longing for the predictable monotony of the workweek to return. Chaos, it seems, can ruin even our relaxation. It is no respecter of weekends or vacations, which can actually be some of the most chaotic events of all. Commotion does not wait for designated space on the calendar. It just appears.

That's not the way I hoped this would go.

Try to plan out your day, and chaos will intervene. Expand that to a five-year plan, and chaos will laugh in your face. Try as we might, our ideas of order and clarity are no match for the entropy built into the universe—dissolving our plans into something messy and muddled, unrecognizable next to our original intentions.

That's not the way I hoped this would go.

Chaotic conditions can go from a trickle to a flood in one fell swoop. From a broken headlight to a broken marriage, a fender bender to a cancer diagnosis. One day it's a bounced check; the next, an economic crash. Or a global pandemic. Or sometimes all of the above.

A virus so contagious that it can creep over unseen

3

during a conversation and infect a friend may spread so widely that it disrupts life on a global level. It can shut down the world at large—global economies, annual events that have never been canceled before, a medical system overwhelmed and scrambling for basic supplies. But we also feel it in the most intimate spaces—someone who lives alone who goes without a hug for months, shelves empty of supplies we've taken for granted, attending a wedding (or even a funeral!) by Zoom, an empty table for a holiday, or an empty church on a holy day. The casualties are indiscriminate in size, the overall chaos so immense we may not know the cost for decades.

That's not the way I hoped this would go.

The Chaos Spectrum

In our own lives, chaos shuffles back and forth from large to small. We are annoyed by minor irritations, devastated by the big picture out of our control. "How are you?" a friend asks. "Doing okay," you say. But you know you're a mess. Pretty quickly your status can escalate from trouble falling asleep to falling apart. When I limp into a staff meeting with wet hair, having slipped in the parking lot and torn the knee of my pants while getting utterly drenched in the downpour in the process, it doesn't help when my coworker chirps, "Cheer up! It could be worse." Forced gratitude or perspective doesn't easily take the edge off. For each of us who are chastised by being told there's someone worse off, there is that someone whose chaos was once minor but who is now repeating the same line to comfort themselves. When will we be them?

When the hurricane of chaos hits, who doesn't long to go back to the breeze of minor irritations? Ask someone whose child has been diagnosed with leukemia if they would prefer the rush of end-of-school-year banquets and buying teacher appreciation gifts over a battery of tests, medical bills, and fears that there won't be another school year to come. Or spend time with someone whose spouse of forty years died in the last few days and see if the annoyance of a rattling snore or the irritation of socks tossed on the floor isn't something they ache for over the silence and empty, bare spaces. I'm sure I would gladly return to the days of the minor disturbance caused by a broken-down fridge if I knew a major loss was looming.

If we stop and reflect, most of us know we're lucky to get by with the small nuisances that chaos throws our way on a daily basis instead of some life-altering bombshell. But that's not usually what's on our minds when the babysitter cancels or the insurance company says it won't cover the treatment we need or our email in-box spills over again into the hours we'd rather not think about it. If prodded, we can recognize that there's always someone worse off, but strangely that doesn't stop the annoyance of gritty irritation from everyday chaos hanging on like sand between our toes.

Landscapes are shaped by the forces of nature around them. Sometimes tectonic plates shift with dramatic and sudden effects. But there's also the stream of water that wears down rock over millions of years until it shapes a canyon—deep and pronounced, so slow that no human eye can detect the changes. Even the gentlest of irritations can shear at our souls. A single, terrible revelation at work might cause you to storm out of your job one day and quit on principle. But a crawling daily commute, lack of recognition for a dozen small projects, and a passive-aggressive boss alongside tiny disagreements with coworkers, and you'd be looking for a new position just the same. Chaos crashes. But it can also rumble just under the surface. Who's to say which is worse when the effect is the same?

What's Your Chaos?

For a period of time, I was so fascinated by the different shapes that chaos takes in people's lives that I'd bring it up in almost every conversation. To chat with me at the grocery store or a neighborhood event meant that I'd eventually find a way to work into the conversation: "So . . . where do *you* experience chaos in your life?" (Yeah, I'm fun at parties.)

As strange a topic for small talk as this might seem, not one person ever looked at me like they had no idea what I was talking about. Really, no one even hesitated. Just the question of chaos in their life immediately triggered a furrow of their brow, a look of disturbed recognition. For some people, the chaos was deeply external—trouble anyone could have identified by looking at their schedule, their medical charts, their financial records, or their home life. For others, it was chaos rumbling within. Worry and anxiety topped the list. Relationships were a close second.

Sometimes chaos outside had seeped into their thoughts, keeping them up at night. Other times, chaos inside was bubbling up and out and affecting their otherwise seemingly ordered outer world. It doesn't seem to matter where the chaos begins. It spreads either way. A chaotic circumstance can ruffle our internal calm. An internal feeling of disturbance starts affecting our external relationships and performance. Unchecked, chaos can have us feeling like we live life in a spin cycle.

In the following pages, we're going to explore every nook and cranny of chaos. We'll talk about its origins, what happens when it's unleashed, and even its hidden gifts. We'll look at where chaos is found in our very human experience—its presence in our co-creating, how it throws us off course, how it leaves us looking for rescue. And we'll talk a lot about the God who creates through chaos, pursues us through it, and equips us to help each other through the ride.

I won't offer you a five-part plan to tackle chaos. I can't promise solutions to vanquish it from your life or control it in the lives of others. This isn't that kind of book. But I will share stories from life and Scripture that tell us just what to expect when we find chaos creeping in again.

There's a chance you've been viewing chaos as the "check engine" light of lost causes, the signal that your life somehow will never measure up. But what if instead chaos was the raw material out of which God creates? In the beginning God converted chaos to order, transforming it into a beautiful creation, and he's been doing it ever since.

Where you and I may experience confusion and disorder, God sees an opportunity for something new—for a rebirth, a renewal, and a renovation. God did this in the beginning and did it again at the cross, and with renewed vision for our disordered world today, we'll look to God to do it again.

PART 1

Origins

Chapter 1

(OUT OF) CONTROL

Nothing seemed out of the ordinary when I slid into the passenger seat and clicked my seat belt. A friend was driving us across town to a restaurant—a place we'd been many times before. Then without warning, we were caught up in a high-speed chase, flying down the highway. Our car barely missed colliding with those around us— careening around corners at a speed I was sure would send us skidding off the road.

I clutched the seat belt to my chest, heart racing, fingers digging into the side of the vinyl seat so deeply I just knew they would leave their outline there. I pressed my foot to an imaginary brake in the floorboard of the passenger side until my leg ached. My eyes stayed glued to the road ahead as if my attention was the only thing keeping us from a certain crash.

Then as suddenly as it began, it was over. My friend pulled smoothly into the parking space and calmly turned off the car, slipping out her door to head into our destination.

It turned out the high speed wasn't in the car; it was in me.

That was as close as I've ever come to a panic attack, and as I stumbled out of the car, dripping with sweat, I couldn't for the life of me figure out where the avalanche of anxiety had come from. All I knew was that I had to figure out how to convince my friend to let me drive home. Whatever chaos had risen up in me was clearly tied to that seat on the passenger side. If there had been no danger on the road, where was it coming from? The answer was both clear and disturbing: it was bubbling up from some place deep within. The speeding was my own heartbeat. The car wasn't out of control at all; I was.

Overtaken by Chaos

What do you do when chaos overtakes you? Panic? Shut down? Scream into a pillow? Escape into numbing substances or actions? Some responses may cause more chaos instead of relieving it. My alternative? To analyze. Take inventory. That's what I did after the high-speed chase that wasn't. I started by interviewing myself like a trauma counselor: Any recent accidents? No. Near misses? None came to mind. When I tried to put my finger on why a simple ride across town suddenly made me fall apart, nothing in my consciousness seemed to offer any answers.

What was so familiar about the emergence of panic and fear in that seat? When had I felt my heart rise into my throat; when had my breathing come at this rapid, shallow pitch; when had I felt so out of control, so helpless? I drew a blank . . . until the next time I clicked my seat belt and felt the feeling of dread settle in my stomach, and something clicked with a recent memory:

Me, on my back.

My legs in the air like a bug that has been tipped over and can't right itself.

My feet pressing into the stirrups until my legs ached —as if I could push an invisible brake pedal down and make it all stop.

My head turning back and forth to look at the ultrasound screen, then at the nurse's guarded face, then back at the screen, longing for a sign of hope on either side—either to catch sight of a tiny, blinking heartbeat or to discover anything on the nurse's face that might reassure me this was all just a nightmare, a bad scare. Heart racing, fingers gripping the vinyl edge of the table, I squeezed my eyes shut as if I could shut out the sound of those words that changed everything: "I'm so sorry, Mrs. LaGrone. There's nothing we can do." Somewhere deep inside where an ultrasound machine could not see, my heart skidded off the road it had been traveling and smashed into a thousand pieces.

When Jim and I married in our thirties, we both knew we wanted children and wanted them soon, and a year into our marriage, the timing seemed perfect. I had just been appointed as one of the pastors at a large church with a day care down the hall from my office. We moved into a new house with more rooms than we needed in a neighborhood filled with families and children. I was giddy when I dropped the packet of birth control into the garbage can, telling myself I'd be pregnant in a month or two. Everything seemed so planned out, so perfectly timed.

Planning, timing, and achieving things was my specialty. Growing up, I learned early that achievers got pats on the head and moved on to the next level to achieve some more. Grades? Check. Leadership? Got it. Extracurriculars? Done. If it was important, I planned it out, timed everything in my life to get perfect results.

I started off my career goals saying I was going to be a doctor, which produced the trifecta of praise from three kinds of people: those who admired intelligence, those who thought it was important to make money, and people who respected careers dedicated to helping others. I was busy basking in approval and knocking down the goals toward medical school when God steered me instead into ministry (so much for the kudos from the admirers of money!). Excited to follow God's will, I was also thrilled to find a new set of goals to achieve: graduate school for a divinity degree, a set of hoops to jump through for ordination in the church, board interviews to pass, and internships to check off. Making goals and reaching them made me feel like I was in the driver's seat in life. Not just accomplished, but safe. Certain.

Like many people, I grew up feeling like I needed to protect myself from chaos. I decided that if things around me weren't predictable and safe, I would create a world I could control. I fought back the forces of chaos from my childhood by trying to build the perfect and predictable life. When my goals for entering the ministry unfolded like clockwork, each requirement ticked off like boxes on a chart, it seemed almost possible to plan the flawless life I'd imagined. I thought everything else would unfold in the same way. Only as my perfect plans for building a family shattered, I felt myself falling back into the well of unpredictability I had once fought so hard to climb out of.

My aspiration to be a mother someday had been a deep desire for most of my life, far surpassing any of the other goals I had already checked off. The timing was finally right. But the months passed after I tossed out the birth control and nothing happened. So, I did what any achiever does best: I made pregnancy my project. I became an expert on the reproductive system. I knew the names of hormones and the stages of follicles, the timing of where every little rise and drop in temperature and symptom should be during the month. And I knew something was wrong. My doctor diagnosed a common syndrome called polycystic ovarian syndrome (PCOS) that keeps ovulation from happening when it's supposed to—or not at all. Medication was prescribed, and our troubles presumed corrected. Again, I just knew that all my planning and careful monitoring would make us parents in no time at all. When chaos interrupts my plans, I'm one of those people who fight back by doubling down. Some call it denial; others call it resiliency. I prefer the latter, I suppose, because I simply respond to the first wave of chaos with resolve. It seemed to work. For a while.

I got my first positive pregnancy test on Jim's birthday. I walked into his office across the hall from our bedroom, still in my pajamas, holding a stick in my hand and looking bewildered. I don't think I ever even said the words, "I'm pregnant." I just held the stick out at him until his face matched my own shocked expression. It was the only birthday present I had ever peed on.

We floated through the next few weeks. Baby names were batted around, and I started eyeing Jim's home office as the next project—a nursery. Just as we were trying to let this news soak in and decide who to tell and when, the bleeding started. Our planning skidded to a halt, commandeered, and instead we were making trip after trip to the doctor's office every other day for tests to find out if the baby would make it. The doctor could give no reassurance if this meant something terrible or nothing at all. We just had to wait and see.

Finally there was that day on the ultrasound table where they found that the embryo's sac, its supposed safe haven, had taken a wrong turn and was forming in my right fallopian tube. They called it an ectopic pregnancy; I called it devastating.

The embryo's detour meant not only an end to any future we had dreamed for this baby, but also a threat to my own life. I frantically Googled treatment options for ectopic pregnancy and found the options discouraging. Whatever course we followed, two lives would be entering the office in one body, and only one of us would be leaving.

We delayed the inevitable as long as we could, so long that my doctor was concerned that a potential rupture could prove life-threatening for me. So we made one last appointment where a shot was administered, and Jim and I were dismissed, hearts dazed and hopes dashed, and told to go home and heal. Do nothing. Wait for my body to recover and come back in a few months. After years of trying, treatments, and a handful of hopeful weeks, being told to wait felt like a prison sentence.

We went home with those words ringing in our ears: *There's nothing we can do.*
Nothing you can do.
Nothing.

The Origins of Chaos

Grief is a form of chaos that finds each of us eventually. Losing someone or experiencing the end of something, no matter how small, throws us into the turmoil of walking through a world that is much the same outside even when we are totally changed inside. Gravity has changed for us. We strain to pull our feet up and take each step, while others continue skipping by. Chaos is the cause of grief. Chaos is also its effect.

Some moments of grief look like the outward chaos of disruption, the unwanted manic phase of denial or keeping so busy that reality has no chance to sink in. In the early days and weeks following a loss, there is no shortage of people to call, decisions to make, things to get done. But alongside that artificial noise, there can be an unnatural level of silence, a period of numbness and sitting in emptiness where someone loved once sat, alone instead of together.

After the empty ultrasound, I woke bleary-eyed each day, hoping for just a moment that my memory wasn't accurate. It always was. I'd go to work at the church where I was a pastor and escape to my office as soon as possible and shut the door. Putting my head down on my desk, I would think to myself, *I should know what to do.* How to make this better. I'm a pastor, for crying out loud! People come to this very office every day and sit on the other side of this desk, expecting me to have the answers. But I had none. My plans, my marriage, my own body—all of these had been commandeered. Hijacked.

I grabbed a Bible from my desk and flipped it open to

the first page. I was so desperate that I resorted to playing Scripture roulette, looking for answers in the first place it cracked open. I didn't know where else to turn. So I read: "In the beginning God created the heavens and the earth. The earth was formless and void, and darkness was over the surface of the deep" (Genesis 1:1–2 NASB 1995).

Some words are so familiar they almost begin to stop making sense. Like a bell that has been rung but doesn't make a sound. I stared at the words on the page, boring holes of desperation, begging them for answers—meaning, anything that would help, anything that would drown out the chaos echoing in the space where joy was just a short time ago. I stared and stared at those opening words until I could almost look right through them.

In the beginning.

Formless and void.

Suddenly I was transported back to a seat in the last row of one of my first seminary classes, hearing the professor saying, "Formless and void. *Tohu vavohu,*" and all of us repeating the Hebrew "*tohu vavohu*" in such a strange monotone that I had almost laughed aloud at the bouncing rhyme of the ancient, unfamiliar words.

This was our introduction to the peculiar language of Old Testament Hebrew, reading from the back of the book to the front, letters running right to left in a counterintuitive flow, more like deciphering a code than learning a language. We tried to read the first few phrases of the Bible aloud with awkward, faltering tongues. *Tohu vavohu.* It sounded so much more like a child's nonsensical rhyme than what it really described—an unformed emptiness bathed in darkness.

Tohu ("formless") gave us a clue to the kind of predeveloped, primordial state of things in the beginning. This was a kind of un-creation, the chaos of a universe without boundaries even to say what it was or was not, where it began or ended.

Vavohu ("and void") showed us that it was empty. Empty of inhabitants, of meaning, of purpose.

This was the backdrop of creation. The block of stone from which everything was chipped. No wonder the universe as we know it tends to slip back into its original state of commotion, causing no end of grief. Chaos is deep in the bones of all we know.

Beginnings are rough sometimes. Every artist knows that the mess comes before the miracle. The universe's beginnings were no exception. Dark and formless and empty, the canvas for creation was muddied and dim.

Unformed. Unfilled. Unlighted.

If you or I had come across the pre-created state at the start of Genesis 1:2 and been told this was the starting point of everything that would ever come into being in the entire universe, we might have just thrown up our hands and given up before passing go. What's the use? These were overwhelmingly inhospitable conditions—an unlivable, watery mess. Unbreathable, lonely, and dark.

But God . . . God loves a challenge. And while there would be many to come, this was the first. A prequel to the many times to come that God and chaos would tango. God gently rolled up his sleeves and, for the first time in recorded history, got to work.

Self-Improvement? Or Self-Acceptance?

If chaos is present from the very beginning, what course can we expect chaos to take in us? The disorder that seems to pop up in mild irritations or the kind that steamrolls our lives into flattened disarray? Bookstores certainly have discovered a market for those of us deep in our own chaos problem. Self-help sections are the largest nonfiction area filling their floor plans. A stroll through these books intended to help a person fix their messy lives (believe me, I've browsed there a few times) reveals a curious divide between two options: either build yourself up through self-improvement or resign yourself to self-acceptance. It would seem contradictory to say you can have *The Life-Changing Magic of Tidying Up* and the startlingly titled book written in response, *The Life-Changing Magic of Not Giving a F****, in the same aisle. Which is it? Do we tidy everything up or let it slide to shambles? Classics like *I'm OK—You're OK* are still selling well, evidently, empowering us to self-acceptance as a means of finding peace in the whirlwind of chaos. But so are books like *The Power of Positive Thinking*, *Getting Things Done*, and *You Can Heal Your Life*, which directly proclaim the opposite: you're definitely not OK, and here's a path to make yourself so.

I've spent most of my life in the self-improvement camp (clearly), working to tweak my five-year plan in a way that will hold back the chaos and create a safe and predictable environment. It didn't work. So what about self-acceptance? Why not just affirm to ourselves, as one self-help title tells us, *You are 10X better than you think you are*, embrace the mess, and slide mercifully into the chaos?

My friend Claire talks about a time in life when she felt that embracing chaos was her only option. Having grown up in a family of dual-alcoholic parents, chaos was like a childhood playmate who was rough but familiar: you might come away bruised, but at least you had someone to play with.

As she approached adulthood, Claire dug deep into delinquency and drugs. She never imagined she would go to college or even leave her hometown, and really didn't expect to live to see twenty-five. She held the record for suspensions from school. When the number of hickeys visible above her collar line became too numerous to count, her mother showed up in the high school cafeteria and handed her boyfriend a pacifier and said, "Here, honey, you can suck on this."

Her local reputation was scandalous. She remembers hearing people whisper about her family and behavior behind her back and thinking to herself, *Oh, you think I'm bad? I'll show you bad.* And she did. The mention of her name at the local high school was said to make teachers shiver and retire early.

She's not sure when her life turned a corner, but at some point, a caring mentor who took an interest in her told her she was smart and had potential to build a different kind of future—two things no previous adult had ever bothered to tell her. A couple of decades later, she finished graduate school, became a minister at a local church, and watched her life transform into one neither she nor anyone who knew her growing up would have even imagined. When someone back home heard the story, they asked her to return to her little hometown to speak at her high school's graduation service. One former teacher greeted her warmly until she discovered that Claire was the keynote speaker for the event and then couldn't hide her disappointment. When Claire was introduced to a couple of local dignitaries sitting on the platform at the graduation ceremony, the wife turned to her husband and said, "You remember Claire, sweetie? She's the one who stole our mailbox."

All these years later, my friend looks back on that chaotic period not with regret but with a kind of curiosity. Why didn't the adults and authority figures ever take a chance and tell her she was capable of a different way of living? Perhaps the pressure to lean into self-acceptance can prevent us from seeing a better self, even in others. The "accept yourself the way you are to find peace" message can translate into "because you're really not capable of rising to anything else." If self-improvement can lead to control issues (ask me how I know), then self-acceptance, in the extreme, may lead to stunted growth and rejected responsibility as we binge on the out-of-control feeling of just letting it all go.

While both self-acceptance and self-improvement are worthy ventures, do they really fix the chaos? Or just hide it under a veneer of white-knuckled hard work or negligent reveling in our own mess? Perhaps the problem with them both is in their root word: *self.* Any path of escaping chaos with self as the central actor inevitably leads us to focus on the self, which circles around until we find ourselves back in a different kind of chaos. Mine was the shattering realization that all the self-improvement and self-control in the world couldn't protect me from the unpredictable. Life in the driver's seat had only been an illusion. Claire's was the opposite: that no-holds-barred self-acceptance meant actually selling herself short. The self's shortsightedness can only expire when we come to the end of ourselves. Facing the fact that our chaos isn't a quick fix, or really isn't ours to fix at all, is perhaps the first step to finding our place in God's creation. Those who have worked their way through the twelve steps of recovery began with this one: we admitted we were powerless. That our lives had become unmanageable. While seemingly a passive admission, taking the self out of self-help is the gateway to God's good work in our lives.

Tohu Vavohu

The formless chaos of Genesis, *tohu vavohu*, was temporary, but God is permanent. Chaos wasn't a formidable foe. It turned out it wasn't even an obstacle but was an entity God could use. God was not in the chaos, and the chaos was not God. This first frame forms a helpful picture for every person staring down the barrel of the confusion and chaos, grief and loss, breakdowns and bedlam. When chaos breaks in, we can confidently declare, *You are not God. You are temporary. You are not the boss of me, and you will not be the end of my story.*

Isaiah the prophet reflects back on the words of Genesis and says, "Yahweh . . . did not create it [the earth] a chaos . . . I did not say . . . 'Look for me in chaos'" (Isaiah 45:18–19).[1] Instead God brought a new reality from the chaos. One that is beyond any acceptance or improvement the self could accomplish. He brought life out of death and light out of darkness. If he could do it with a universe-sized project, surely our little wells of chaos, no matter how deep, are places he can work in as well.

Those first paragraphs of Scripture, opened in a mess of tears and desperation on my desk, were the beginning of a rope I would grab hold of and cling to for dear life. The day I stumbled over *tohu vavohu* and watched light and order and fullness appear out of those words, it seemed like Providence that led me to them. But I could have opened the Bible to any page and seen these same three actions: ordering chaos, filling emptiness, and lighting darkness.

Every action God takes, every step toward the creation he loves, is designed to fulfill these purposes: order, fullness, light. We can watch them unfold from page 1 onward. They infuse the law given to help people stay out of the well of chaos. They echo in the warning words of prophets admonishing people who are chasing chaos's tail. They sing out in stories and in psalms. And when we finally crack the spine between Old and New Testaments and turn to the story where God's name is known as Jesus, his actions, his teachings, his miracles, his relationships—they all echo the purposes of God in this first moment of creation: order, fullness, and light. Each person Jesus meets finds that chaos subsides at his touch. If anyone is in Christ, behold: new creation![2] And so it all starts over again.

Is it silly to say I clung to three little words in the first paragraph of the Bible to get me through my hardest days? That they opened my eyes to recognize disorder, void, and darkness as if I had slept with them as my blanket every night? That I longed for order, fullness, and light like I had never longed for, never worked to achieve, anything else? I think part of me just needed to hear that the chaos was not all in my head. Or in my body. That it was not just in me at all.

If we believe the first chapter of the Bible, then chaos is in the bones of this place. Down in the bedrock. When we're hijacked by chaos, it feels deeply unique and personal, as if we were the first one smacked by the harshness of life. In reality, experiencing chaos is probably one of the most common things we face. Instead of pushing us to the edges—divided, peculiar, and alone—shared chaos has the power to bring us together, common travelers on a road we didn't choose.

Chaos existed from the very beginning. But the chaos doesn't rule. Instead, it is ruled. It doesn't remain as it is, nor does it disappear, but it is changed. God is not afraid of chaos, emptiness, and darkness. These are ingredients he uses to make beautiful things. When these murky gifts pop up in our lives, we can hand them over in surrender and find God rolling up his sleeves to start something beautiful again.

This dark and murky beginning gives us hope that maybe God can claim even the worst chaos for his grand purposes. Maybe the world isn't spinning out of control, but it's on a potter's wheel. The forces of chaos, as hard as they may whirl, can be shaped and guided by an artist's hand.

I've never liked being the clay. Never liked the passenger seat. I'd much rather drive. But I don't think God is inviting us to let chaos rule or run our lives. It was never intended to take a place behind the wheel.

We know now how it started. Where will it end up? Where will *we* end up? Seat belts clicked, fingers gripped on the sides of the seat, we hang on and wait to find out.

Chapter 2

WHEN ORDER AND CHAOS COLLIDE

It's in the kitchen that you find out who you really married. You learn whether your spouse is a stickler for expiration dates, whether they leave dishes to soak in the sink for hours or clean them as they go, whether they drink straight from the carton or abide by rules upon rules about how to properly load a dishwasher.

They say conflict stirs in most marriages around major decisions like child-rearing, money, and whose family to visit on major holidays. But anyone who has ever tried to fit two lives into one knows that the true testing ground in any relationship is the kitchen.

Eating and food preparation may seem inconsequential in the scheme of things, but they are repetitive and unavoidable details of life. Food is a resource most couples combine right away, even if bank accounts stay separate and the perennial argument about thermostat setting in winter can be put off for a few months. Food comes up early and often, bringing frequent opportunities to disagree.

Decisions about what to eat, how it will be prepared, and by whom must be made three times a day, so tiny choices about whether to order Papa John's Pizza or Domino's Pizza can make or break a relationship way before any major pronouncements are made about whether to vacation in the mountains or the beach, to spend or save, to move around or stay put.

A few blissful months into my newlywed life with Jim,
our moment of kitchen truth came. It was the infamous day
we both got a hankering for some macaroni and cheese.
"Mmmm . . . *real* macaroni and cheese?" Jim clarified
over the combined rumbling of our stomachs.

"Definitely!" I said, and we rushed together to the
kitchen, where he searched the refrigerator for five cheeses
and cream to start a roux, and I reached to the back of the
pantry for the blue box—the box containing *real* macaroni
and cheese, complete with the *real* fluorescent orange pow-
der tucked away inside.

When we turned and found each other holding very different ingredients, it was as if we had each discovered alien
life beamed down into our kitchen. Who *was* this person?

It was then I knew we might have a problem.

I had unwittingly married someone from one of *those*
families—the ones who make everything from scratch.
There had never been a box of Hamburger Helper or a
Stouffer's Lasagna with Meat & Sauce anywhere near the
kitchen where Jim grew up—and it was showing. We were
evidently born into households on the opposite sides of the
kitchen world.

On one side are the cooking-from-scratch people. Like
hunters and gatherers, they scour the grocery store aisles
(or even better, the farmers market) for things labeled
"fresh" and "whole," such as an actual vanilla bean from
which to extract flavor. They spend hours chopping, mari-
nating, preheating, and prepping and then emerge to place
steaming platters on the table like an offering on the altar.

And then there's the other kind of cooks—a club in

which I cannot disguise my membership. We don't really think much about food until we get hungry. Then we start asking ourselves things like, *I wonder if we've got any Hot Pockets left in the back of the freezer.* When it comes to dinner, we're much more likely to start with a mix—or even maybe a takeout menu.

The family I grew up in had an unspoken kitchen philosophy that was something like this: "If God made a mix for that, it was his way of telling me I shouldn't have to start from scratch. Praise God from whom all Betty Crocker flows!"

By contrast, Jim's family instilled in him a different kind of kitchen philosophy: "If I could start from scratch, why would I use a mix?"

Jim's cooking from scratch went beyond dinner to things like biscuits, ice cream, and bread. I'll admit this new world was tasty for me, but I discovered that he even made his own granola bars. He even made his own granola. I didn't even know where granola came from. Twigs?

We continued to banter over things like whether emptying a pouch in a bowl and adding a couple of eggs and oil actually counted as *baking* a cake, but more and more, my side of these arguments came through muffled mouthfuls of homemade goodies Jim continued to hand me, saying, "Here, try this." Eventually my arguments just ceased altogether, and I conceded—and have been eating my words (deliciously!) ever since.

As much as I enjoy Jim's creative work in the kitchen, I still tease him that no human being has ever really started from scratch.

Carl Sagan put it well: "If you wish to make an apple

pie from scratch, you must first invent the universe."[3] You and I can never really start from scratch because we can never really make something out of nothing. All of our raw ingredients are the outcomes of a recipe that God started long ago, the familiar recipe that begins, "In the beginning God created the heavens and the earth" (Genesis 1:1).

Systematic and Orderly

In triune love, God doesn't create beauty in order to hoard it for himself. He doesn't order chaos to create a sterile, controlled environment void of liveliness or laughter. He orders creation so that he can fill it and share it—so that life will bubble and ebb and flow and fidget its way through the days of life that will come, evening and morning, the next day and the next and the next. Witnessing God's first acts as Cosmic Chef at the counter of creation may help us see it all from his perspective, or as much as that is possible, peeking over God's shoulder as he mixes and measures, folds and kneads chaos into creation, anticipating the day when we will enjoy all that he has made.

How does God begin the universe? He simply utters, "Let there be light," and the universe is flooded with it. The awesome power of God's words, his gift of speaking to create, will only amaze us more as the steps of creation unfold. Words fall from God's lips, and worlds come into being. From chaos to cosmos, just like that. God doesn't break a sweat. He orders up worlds with words like we'd order up a latte—with better results. I could say, "Let there be almond milk," and it could still go wrong. God says, "Let there be everything," and it is so.

With God's words, darkness and light are now separate, distinct states. And here's something worth holding on to, a hopeful handle for everyone who will ever feel dark or danger, depression or deep distress; here's where it becomes utterly clear that darkness is not of God. *It is separate from him.* God is separate from the darkness, but he's also present in it. He's not frightened of it, not afraid to walk right up to it and command it. Darkness—which will haunt humankind in many forms—is simply an ingredient to God. Something to be shaped and formed for the greater recipe to come. This is a message passed forward in time for when we will wonder if rough waters will prevail: Take heart. God is not confounded by chaos. He is *in* the chaos with us!

The lights now on, God turns to the formless void. This is the *tohu vavohu.* The vague, primordial chaos. A black hole of wild and waste. The nothing that comes before the something that will be our everything.

Commanding the formless void, God begins to form order from chaos. Calling forth order means separating. Day by day, God separates out one thing from the next, distinguishing them from each other.

Day 1: separating light and darkness, day and night
Day 2: separating sky above and waters below
Day 3: separating land and seas

Separating is a part of ordering anything. To conquer my unruly desk, I begin by separating papers into piles.

We organize piles of laundry into piles of lights and darks. We put away groceries in categories—cans here, snacks here, refrigerated things here. Without separating and distinguishing, our lives are easily buried, soiled, and spoiled.

With the act of separating, God also creates time. Separating one day from the next with the words "there was evening, and there was morning—the first day" gives the days both boundaries and identities, but it also connects them, ties them together as a series of days that will be both distinct and connected. Boundaries determine where one ends and another begins.

Separating and sorting is good news, for God doesn't create an indistinct soup of beings whose edges are so blurred they cannot be distinguished one from another. All of us have known someone who forgot where their business ended and ours began. Take away boundaries and we become controlling and judgmental, or helpless and dependent. God's gift of separation means that light is not darkness, sky is not sea, land is not water. But it also gives the gift of meeting and mingling. It's at the margins where the dance begins, as waves crash onto land and sunrise turns night into day. These differences make life beautiful.

God transformed existence from unruly, chaotic bedlam to welcoming homes structured by cosmic constants ready to be filled—empty but anticipating what will come. Formlessness and void are ready to be formed and filled. These acts are the antidotes to chaotic emptiness.

Even the way the story unfolds echoes the creation it describes, precise and orderly. The first three days, God forms environments; the next three, he fills them with inhabitants. The two movements, formed and filled, line up side by side as we see God's blueprints grow.

Day 1: the environment of light and dark	Day 4: filled with inhabitants of sun, moon, and stars
Day 2: environment of sky above and water below	Day 5: filled with inhabitants of birds and fish
Day 3: environment of dry land separate from the sea	Day 6: filled with inhabitants of animals and, finally, humans

These carefully ordered environments are filled with teeming life—inhabitants that run and swim and soar, those who bring unspeakable possibilities and the excitement of stories yet to be written. Formed and filled, God's earth made God's way with God's glorious recipe, all for us to enjoy. *Bon appétit.*

Sometimes when we tell this story of a good and loving God who gathers and separates creation into such order, the flavor comes out wrong. We may begin to hear the story of God speaking chaos into order as a kind of fussy housekeeper, more concerned with keeping things neat in the world he creates than with the lives of those he has placed to dwell there. My mother, who was an elementary school librarian before she retired, used to spend weeks each summer getting her library organized and decorated and ready for the start of the school year. You could hold a ruler to the books, they were lined up so straight at the end of the shelves. Once the room was ready, she would sometimes take a step back to survey her work and say with teasing irony, "The library would stay really nice if we could just keep the kids out." Couldn't the same be said of God's creation?

If God is a persnickety creator who covers all the furniture in plastic and follows behind us, wiping our sticky fingerprints off the walls, then what good is a good world, since we must constantly be on our guard about messing it up all the time? Can a God who delights in order love messy people?

Messy People in an Ordered World

My friend Ryanne is a colorful Christian. Her home is colorful. She often paints a wall or ceiling or the whole front porch on a whim, based on some color that has drawn her fancy. Her family is colorful. Her children's skin colors are a glorious variety of hues. Her language is sometimes a little colorful. As she stands yelling at her four kids and two dogs (and yardful of chickens, to boot) from her multicolored porch, she sometimes uses words that attract attention and occasional alarm from her aging neighbors. She stands out in her neighborhood, and pretty much everywhere else, which is clearly the way Ryanne likes it.

She especially stands out when she and her kids pull into the church parking lot on Sundays, her ancient station wagon covered in bumper stickers that range from humorous and whimsical to edgy and political, surrounded by all the matching minivans. It can be hard at first to tell who the adult is in this brood. Ryanne is shorter than her oldest and matches him in cropped hair and faded jeans. She looks a little more like a teen headed to detention than a mother of four on her way to worship. Her church attire is a special T-shirt—one of her favorites to wear to church has *I love Jesus, but I cuss a little* printed across the front. "Just because I don't dress like a church lady doesn't mean I don't believe like one," she laughs.

Does someone whose life seems so messy fit into the orderly picture of God's good creation?

Honestly, Ryanne has one of the most solid faiths of anyone I've ever met. Her house and car might look a little odd, but she and Jesus are tight. He was with her when the child support was late again. When the electricity was about to be turned off. When her middle kid wanted to go live with his dad. When her daily life was as torn and beat-up as the old carpet on her back porch, where we sat as she told me how Jesus helped her put the pieces back together.

Just because he made her whole again didn't mean he ironed her personality flat.

One mistake we make is to assume God's call to order is a sentence to bland uniformity. He didn't tidy up the vast expanse of creation expecting us to fall marching into line. Looking around at the world he made, we can see that his creativity is unmatched. Whether or not we wear it on our T-shirts, all of us are a little colorful, made up of stories and opinions pasted over a bit with life and humor and politics that would entertain some and shock others.

But God's idea of order in this vast universe wasn't

meant to keep the riffraff out, to place plastic covers on the couches, or to send uniform Christian soldiers trooping into churches dressed up and combed up and polished into essentially the same model with a slightly different minivan.

The design of order in creation was never meant to decree uniformity. Creation by separation was never meant to make clubs of those who belong and outcasts of those who don't. There's no sign or secret handshake that Christians have to give in order to be truly accepted. The mark of a life lived faithfully with Christ isn't some outwardly visible thing that shows up in our homes, our dress, or the shape of our family portraits in the church directory. It doesn't matter if you wear a suit or a faded T-shirt. Those are only outward appearances, after all, and God looks at the heart.

Good Things Run Wild

In my late twenties, I took my first mission trip, leaving the United States for the mountains of Costa Rica, where I fell in love with the people and the incredible views. I was definitely unskilled labor at the tasks our group had signed up for—mixing concrete with a shovel and setting the foundation of what would be two new houses, projects of an international chapter of Habitat for Humanity. Instead, my best work was building relationships with the children of the village, who laughed at my toddler-level Spanish and taught me simple games on the rocky hillside.

One day, a group of them shyly pulled me by the hand

and told me they were going to show me the most beautiful place on their mountain, a claim that piqued my interest, since this was already the most beautiful place I had ever seen.

After a long and breathless hike, we finally turned a corner where I saw, in the middle of all the rugged mountainous glory . . . a lawn. A simple, flat lawn, rockless and sprawling, just like thousands of green suburban landscapes back home.

To put it bluntly, I was underwhelmed.

Just then, one of the boys pulled out a ball, and they began running and kicking it with glee. This space, while it looked like an ordinary neighborhood front yard to me, was their soccer field (*fútbol* to them)—the only one for miles around. To them it was holy ground.

G. K. Chesterton's take on the discipline and order found in the Christian life was that "the more I considered Christianity, the more I found that while it had established a rule and order, the chief aim of that order was to give room for good things to run wild."[4]

When God, on the first three days of creation, laid out one environment after another, creating space to swim and fly, to run and walk, to breathe and sing and dance, he was preparing a space ordered for the things that would come to live in it. When he looked out at each created space and named it "good," surely part of the goodness was the intended purpose—the goodness to come, as wild things, humanity included, would enjoy this place to its fullest.

There is something appealing about order, about pristine gardens and manicured lawns. Why risk letting anyone in to mess it up? If order is the highest value, then why allow play? Put up signs on the field that read, "Keep Off the Grass!" Fertilize it to green perfection. Manicure the heck out of it. Mow it in careful parallel stripes and guard it from pests, especially those big enough to run and kick a soccer ball.

Form is beautiful. Fullness is messy. What does it say about God that he didn't put a plastic cover on the couch of creation? That he didn't put up a "Keep Off the Grass" sign and shake his fist every time we came near?

We've bought into the lie that there are only two options: to either keep everyone off the field so they won't mess it up, or to let it all go to seed, to descend into a wild space overtaken by weeds. The creation story paints a shocking alternative. God took the dark, empty chaos and made a beautiful space. Then instead of hiding it away, he decided to share it with us, knowing that our footprints would mess the field but that our play would be the ultimate fullness, the thing he made it all for.

Room to Play

Sometimes we tell ourselves the lie that the life God loves is a sterile, empty picture of life where there's no room for human error. But anything that doesn't allow room for human error doesn't allow room for humans, and the whole point of the creation recipe culminates in putting humans in the environment to flourish in their relationship with God and each other.

I once attended a dinner where a popular Christian writer spoke, her body colorfully illustrated with tattoos and her talk peppered with profanity. The audience loved it. During the Q and A time at the end, someone asked, "What spiritual disciplines do you practice?" She drew herself up and locked eyes with the audience over her dark-rimmed glasses for effect before replying, "I don't do *shit*." After a dramatic pause, she added, "I don't need a checklist to work my way up some ladder to God's standards. God doesn't need me to be anything but what I already am." People applauded loudly. I sat wondering if those who assumed that the spiritual acts of prayer, worship, and engaging Scripture were constricting had ever experienced them as moments of freedom, of joy, of finding oneself at home in the presence of God?

If we are using the twin motivators of shame and achievement to admonish others to read the Bible faithfully or pray regularly, to worship or to serve, we're doing it wrong. Spiritual practices are no ladder to reach God. What if they're actually a form of play? What if they're the field God has created for us to run and laugh with him? If we "don't do shit," how will we encounter him? Where will he meet with us? Maybe he's standing at the corner of the field holding the ball, waiting for the fun to start.

The playing field God provides for us in Scripture doesn't exist to constrain his creation or cramp our style, but to provide the room for "good things to run wild," as G. K. Chesterton celebrated—a clear and free space for living that means our flourishing, the restoration of his image in us and his glory in creation, and a place for goodness to run wild in our communion together. God's children bringing their imperfect and chaotic selves into his presence to commune with him is just the glorious chaos he ordered. A creation empty of messy inhabitants would be a different kind of chaos—the chaos of puritanical sterility, lacking the vulnerability that always comes when we open ourselves to sharing life and space with others.

Signs of Life

When life comes pouring in, all kinds of accompanying miracles and mayhem come with it, even in places we wouldn't expect. That's exactly what happened when Dr. Bill Thomas became the new medical director at Chase Memorial Nursing Home in New Berlin, New York.

When Dr. Thomas arrived at Chase Memorial Nursing Home, he found a tidy, well-run facility. The staff there were focused on keeping patients safe and comfortable in their last years of life, and they were doing it well. But Thomas noted that while the environment was quiet and safe, the light had gone out in many people's eyes. The excellent job the caregivers had done in providing order and minimizing risk had also succeeded in producing a dead calm.

Dr. Thomas began to wonder what it would look like not just to keep patients alive, but to give them a reason for living. He wanted Chase to feel like a real home, not an institution. He found the inspiration for what was missing when he went home at night to his own household: plants, animals, and children—untidy, unpredictable, and utterly alive.

The plan Thomas formulated and presented to the administration was called, appropriately, the Eden Alternative. If you've been imagining the Garden of Eden as a serene and tranquil paradise, you might not have pictured every kind of creature bursting onto the scene with all of their predatory and procreative instincts revved up and ready to go. As the old Lucky Strike cigarette ad used to quip, "Nature in the raw is seldom mild."[5]

Dr. Thomas first proposed removing all the artificial plants and adding live plants in every room of the facility. He wanted to pull up the back lawn and plant vegetable and flower gardens. Then he proposed housing one dog and two cats on each of the home's two floors. He was going to have to lobby the forces at the state capitol for waivers to work around the rules and regulations that stipulated no more than a single pet per nursing home. But the menagerie was only getting started. Thomas proposed a flock of laying hens and a colony of rabbits on the grounds. A hundred parakeets in cages would be brought into living areas and residential rooms.

Oh, and he wanted the staff to bring their kids to work so they could spend time around the residents too, and he proposed opening an after-school program for the community.

Surprisingly, the administration signed off on the proposal—mostly because they assumed Thomas would never get the approval he needed from the authorities to put his plan in action. How wrong they were. Dr. Thomas was awarded not only the grant money he needed to accomplish the plan but also all the waivers needed for the rules he wanted to bend. Now they were going to have to see if it all worked.

The residents at Chase Nursing Home had been existing in a *tohu vavohu*—a state empty of light and life. The staff's efforts to produce a calm, safe environment added up to an empty existence that actually accelerated the end of life for many residents rather than giving them something to keep living for. This little corner of creation had order but no fullness. It was formed, but not filled. But all that was about to change.

The prescribed dose of what Dr. Thomas had gleefully called "total pandemonium" arrived so quickly that no one was really prepared for the consequences.[6] A greyhound named Target and a lapdog named Ginger were both getting settled amicably on their separate floors, figuring out how to share space with two cats each. Staff members' children were dropped off at the door by their school buses each afternoon. The back lawn was dug up and transformed into a garden and a playground next to the rabbit pen and chicken coop. Things were getting a bit crowded.

And then, in the midst of it all, the birds arrived. One hundred parakeets, all delivered on one day in one truckload—with the birdcages nowhere to be seen. The staff locked all one hundred birds in the center's hair salon until the cages arrived later the same day—some assembly required. Through the glass picture windows of the hair salon, the residents gathered, watching and laughing as the staff spent hours assembling birdcages and chasing the loose parakeets all over the hair salon, grabbing at feathers and ducking as birds flapped around their heads. "Glorious chaos" had arrived.[7]

The pandemonium caused by all these changes was not all humorous. I can tell you personally from years of helping to stage live nativity scenes in the back parking lot of our church each December: when you get live children and live animals together, there's no telling what's going to happen. The staff pushed back at times on their new duties. Some felt that if money could be spent on animals, then someone should be hired to care for them all. But gradually, someone else did begin to take over the animals' care—namely, the residents.

Many of the elderly residents agreed to host a pair of parakeets in their rooms. They helped water the hundreds of new indoor plants and demanded a say in the planting of the flower and vegetable gardens. Residents who had previously been nonambulatory said they'd take one of the dogs outside for a walk. Light began to dawn in people's eyes. Even some of those with advanced forms of dementia seemed to take joy in the burgeoning life and noise around them. They could recognize birdsong, run their fingers through a pet's fur, turn their head when a child ran shrieking down the hall.

Over the first two years of Chase's Eden Alternative, researchers watched the center's vital signs carefully. Their study found that the number of medicines being prescribed at Chase fell by half, especially those prescribed for agitation. The number of deaths fell by 15 percent. The immeasurable changes were even easier to witness: life came back into residents' eyes, and the number of smiles grew daily. Instead of simply waiting for death, they were jolted back to life as it ran and chirped, hopped, and grew all around them.

Forming and filling turned out to be a great recipe for life, not just in the first Eden, but even in the midst of those gathering for the last years of their lives. It's a recipe that God started from scratch, but it was meant to be repeated in us too, for good things to run wild from the countertop of God's creation into each of our lives, as holy and messy as the day is long.

Chapter 3

CHAOS UNLEASHED

It was early March 2020. I had just begun to collect my thoughts on chaos into what I hoped would become a book when the world fell apart.

At first, the signs of chaos fell like a few fat drops of rain falling and landing with a "plink"—one or two, here and there—enough to turn my head but not especially disruptive. But as I began to pay attention, signs pointing to chaos multiplied until it became a deluge pouring out everywhere. Every conversation, every headline, every story overflowed with chaos, the drops turning into a downpour. I couldn't hear anything else over the noise.

A virus so new that none of us had ever even heard its name trickled into our consciousness and then ripped across borders until it was everywhere, from large cities to tiny hometowns. Soon it was a household word: COVID-19. With it, chaos ran rampant through bloodstreams, hospitals, nations. It permeated every news story, every conversation.

The illness caused one kind of chaos, the attempted treatment another. We normally think of chaos as a rush of hectic, disorganized overactivity—an out-of-control presence. Our attempts to fight the virus introduced a new kind of chaos—absence. In our small town, things got really quiet really fast. The stores and restaurants sported "closed" signs, and the schools shut their doors. I watched out our front window as families passed by on their daily walks and hurriedly crossed the street if someone approached, avoiding even saying hello. Our family holidays were canceled for the first time in even my ninety-nine-year-old grandmother's lifetime, and even she began to learn Zoom and FaceTime just so she could see her loved ones.

Who would have imagined that chaos could look like an aching hole that all of life's activities had left behind? It was an entire season of forfeit, the time we all lost something, big or small, that a virus took from us. COVID stole loved ones, jobs and businesses, social contact, and a sense of security, leaving many feeling helpless and aching for some faraway state everyone wanted to get back to called "normal."

The floodwaters of chaos continued to rise. In the United States, racial injustice, tense elections, dueling information sources, and violence shouted across headlines: "Chaos at the Capitol! Chaos in the Streets! Chaos in Hospital Wards!" As communities and nations drifted in and out of lockdowns, neighbors stood apart, divided by fear of contagion and sharp lines of political disagreement.

Each generation of human history experiences an era when chaos seems to run rampant, and this was ours. The world was drowning in it. These were unprecedented times. At least, that's how people started their emails then: "I hope you and your family are well in these unprecedented times," they opened. Closings changed from "Sincerely" to "Stay safe!"

With my head already buried deep in chaos I wondered, *Was this really so unprecedented? Had chaos really just appeared out of nowhere—or had it begun long ago?* What if the global pandemic of chaos had begun snaking its way through our bloodstreams, across our borders, before any diagnostic tools existed to name it or mark its spread? What if long before the word *virus* ever entered our vocabulary (or even before the discovery of microorganisms for that matter), chaos had snuck into our reality, insidious and invisible, and invaded humanity from the inside out?

What on Earth Happened?

The pages of Genesis first traced the progress of God as he ordered creation step-by-step, separating light and dark, sky and sea, water and land. Then it described how he filled each of those spaces with the inhabitants meant to beautifully run wild in their environments, bringing earth alive with the joy of God's good creation. If the story continued on this trajectory, we would look around us and see a perfectly ordered world with no chaos in sight. We would gaze on the headlines, the relationships, the events of our world, and exclaim as God did in Genesis, "It is very good!"

But if you're like me, those aren't the words that escape your lips when you survey the world! You may have paused from time to time, looking around and wondering, *What on earth happened!* Our world shows so many signs of darkness, chaos, and emptiness creeping back in. It's not just news headlines that reveal a broken world, but also (more personally) glimpses into the lives of those around us that show broken lives, broken homes, broken hearts.

Origin Stories

In the comic books, heroes and villains all have their origin stories. If someone is remarkably strong or fast or evil, it always provokes the question: How did they get this way? Whether they were bitten by a radioactive spider and end up slinging webs from tall buildings or a terrible accident left their face frozen in a horrible, lopsided grin as if they're always making a sick joke, knowing their origin stories helps us understand and follow how our favorites or foes became who they are.

Genesis unpacks origin stories of both the good and the bad. The world of Eden is made by a God whose words spoke worlds into being. But the events that transpired afterward reveal the cracks of chaos spreading through this good world in such a devastating trajectory that we are still experiencing the aftershocks.

The cracks of chaos began with a tiny fruit, eaten by humans who picked the one forbidden choice over the countless good ones. While this little snapshot may seem inconsequential in world history, it is actually this first hiccup of sin that still reverberates through our world today, a single choice seemingly tiny but significant for all of humanity. How is this possible?

The Butterfly Effect

Small differences end up making huge impacts. Back in 1961, a meteorologist by the name of Edward Lorenz

53

made a profound discovery about how small differences in input can lead to vastly different outcomes. Lorenz was using a very early model of a computer (the ones where people fed in punch cards to enter data into machines that took up entire rooms) to work on some data for weather forecasting. He decided to go back and rerun a few of the models he was working on, but instead of going all the way back to the beginning, he started at a later point, taking what he thought were the same numbers and entering them, starting in the middle of the process to save time. While the numbers he entered were the same, they weren't as specific as the originals, going only to three decimal places instead of six. When he came back later, he was shocked to find that the forecasted outcomes were wildly different. Lorenz called the impact that tiny differences have on vast outcomes "chaos theory." A simplification of the theory explains that in weather forecasting, just the flap of a tiny butterfly's wing might end up creating a hurricane on the other side of the world. This was the hallmark of a chaotic system—small differences resulting in catastrophic effects.

Many of us learned about chaos theory under the less than scientific auspices of the 1990s action blockbuster *Jurassic Park*. In it, a scientist played by the iconic Jeff Goldblum warns that creating an island filled with flesh-eating dinosaurs might not be such a good idea, no matter how many safety measures are in place, because through the tiny cracks of chaos "life finds a way."[8] As anyone who saw even five minutes of the movie knows, he was right.

Chaos theory simply means predicting that things will

happen in an unpredictable fashion. It doesn't take an actor playing a chaotician to know this is a pretty safe bet.

In life, as in the movies, the human story is filled with these kinds of outcomes. Where God planted good, the tiny seed of sin has fallen alongside and grown chaos on a scale that's hard to comprehend. The actions of people, from eating the fruit in the Garden of Eden onward, have shaped history, sometimes catastrophically. It doesn't take being chased down by a flesh-eating T-Rex to know that chaos will find a way.

Global chaos is sometimes unleashed on a scale so broad we cannot comprehend it, but sometimes it's as local as our own living rooms.

As a group of moms were sitting around talking about the challenges of parenting, a friend admitted that she yells at her children. We all do, of course, but she was the first to confess. She even admitted to the specific phrase that sometimes pops out.

"What the hell!" she yells. In context it makes complete sense:

She discovers a potted plant lying on the ground, pot broken and dirt spilling out across the carpet. The guilty parties have left the scene of the crime.

What the hell!

She walks into a kitchen that was clean just a few hours earlier but is now in total disarray, dishes piled with half-eaten food on the counters, milk left out to spoil.

What the hell!

She intervenes in a fight between multiple siblings, more than one of them injured and crying and all pointing a finger at someone else for starting it.

What the hell!

All the parents nod in recognition. Hell has crept into our households too. We've all gaped in astonishment at how something we've worked so hard to order has been trashed.

What the hell! How did it get in again? Who left the door open this time?

This is chaos on a tiny spectrum, seemingly innocuous to anyone except those heroes who work on a daily basis to restore order by putting the same dishes away, folding the same laundry, scooping the same soil into the potted plant that was turned over yet again.

The same relatable mom who walks around restoring hell to heaven in the wake of her five children also told us about a work training she attended recently to prepare her for some situations that were utterly unrelatable. She travels internationally for a large company and is often sent into situations that may or may not be dangerous. Life-threatening, even. At her company's recent training, former Navy SEALS (now consultants) were brought in to explain what to do if they were kidnapped for ransom or political leverage, or if they found themselves under fire from terrorists. Between answering texts from her kids about what leftovers they were allowed to heat up for lunch, she found herself on her belly, army crawling and rolling sideways, learning how to stay low on her escape route if incoming fire from terrorists was coming in just over her head.

Hell travels quickly from the playroom to the board-room. If the goal of faith is not just to get us into heaven but to get heaven into us, then hell has an equally incarnate path—hatred gone viral in human hosts, spilling out to disorder the good world we were meant to live in.

Flooded with Chaos

While the first cracks of sin emerged early in the Genesis story, within just a few chapters of human history they have spread outward into an all-encompassing outcome: "The LORD saw how great the wickedness of the human race had become on the earth, and that every inclination of the thoughts of the human heart was only evil all the time" (Genesis 6:5)

How could something that started with a tiny fruit end up going global? What begins with a butterfly's wing sometimes ends up as a hurricane.

Great wickedness. *Every* inclination. *Only* evil. *All* the time.

Sin, like a virus, had spread until it had reached every corner, every person, every thought and motive and inclination—and it didn't take a break. There was no flattening the curve of infection. It dominated thoughts and actions, relationships, and systems. Humanity's cruelty, depravity, and corruption revealed a world of chaos in full flower.

As the virus coursed unchecked through the veins of every human being, infection spilled over from earth's inhabitants to the environment around them. The primordial waters, once boundaried back to make breathing room for life to flourish, now crashed back together and flooded the earth with watery chaos.

A prophet once wrote about this interconnectedness of sin flooding through inhabitants and their environment in verse with familiar echoes:

> "My people are fools;
>> they do not know me.
> They are senseless children;
>> they have no understanding.
> They are skilled in doing evil;
>> they know not how to do good."
> I looked at the earth,
>> and it was formless and empty;
> and at the heavens,
>> and their light was gone.
> I looked at the mountains,
>> and they were quaking;
>> all the hills were swaying.
> I looked, and there were no people;
>> every bird in the sky had flown away.
> I looked, and the fruitful land was a desert;
>> all its towns lay in ruins
>> before the LORD, before his fierce anger.
>
> *Jeremiah 4:22–26*

Formless and empty. Environments destroyed. Inhabitants disappeared. There's no clearer message that *tohu vavohu* has returned. The description of a land returning to chaotic desert, empty of inhabitants, rings an unwelcome and all-too-familiar bell.

The bright spot within it all was the hope carried by

one human family. Perhaps things could be different with them. Noah and his family rode out the storm in a boat built on faithfulness. Their charge was to plant and spread goodness over the newly washed earth. God even sent a wash of color as a promise sign that this was the last time the earth would be overwhelmed in exactly this way.

But once the waters subsided, it became clear that this family would also be carriers of the same deep sickness. How devastating to find that those who were hoped to be pilgrims of holiness had carried the virus into the new world on the other side of the storm! It didn't take long for the symptoms to manifest themselves. Even as they began again to multiply and cover the earth, the virus would be multiplying too, an unwelcome stowaway riding along into new frontiers.

Running toward Chaos

The year that chaos ripped through the world I lived in, I pondered the headlines, the rising curve of infection, the increasing reports of friends whose family members became sick and those who had died. Many experienced chaos up close and personal. No life was immune to disruption, but for some, it was the season they met disaster.

Looking back at the original cracks in creation, I could see a faint possibility. Instead of a breakdown of God's good plans for the earth, perhaps these super-spreading circles of destruction showed confirmation of its design. A world that runs against God's plan naturally runs toward chaos.

The missionary E. Stanley Jones wrote, "Revolt against God and a resulting chaos work out as prophecy and fulfillment, as seed and fruit. We cannot live on a collectively selfish basis without having a collective clash."[9]

This is how God made the world from the beginning. To run toward order and light. Anything that runs backward toward chaos sends the whole system into rewind. To work determinedly against the fabric of the good world God has made damages that fabric, even as we do damage to ourselves and each other.

Running in Reverse

Years before, I was in a meeting with the staff at the large church where I was a pastor. We were planning that year's Good Friday service, an annual extravaganza that rivaled even Easter and Christmas celebrations. As usual, we'd have a fish fry, games, a bounce house, and a petting zoo (because nothing says "Jesus died for you" quite like a bounce house and petting zoo), but on that planning night, we were focusing on the worship service itself. We were determined to make a video for the Good Friday service that would be unforgettable. Usually our Good Friday videos featured short stories illustrating how people's lives were visibly made better by encountering the cross. But this year, we wanted to go bigger. We wanted to show not just the individual impact of the cross in our personal journeys but the global, overall effect of Jesus' death and resurrection. Someone on the team suggested using 2 Corinthians 5:17 as our guide: "If anyone is in Christ, the new creation has come." How do we show that in a video? How will we communicate creation starting all over again?

We sat for a little while and then an idea began to emerge. We would try to show the impact of sin on the world on a much bigger scale. We would show images of famine and war and devastation. Acid rain would kill trees; plagues would decimate populations; rainforests would be cut down. Anytime we could find historical footage, we would put that in there too: the Hindenburg would explode; Hitler would rise to power; Martin Luther King Jr. would be assassinated; bombs would be dropped. We would show the long, spiraling descent of the earth into chaos.

And then after all that, we would show the cross. Jesus breathing his last breath. The tomb. The lights would completely go out.

After a pause for dramatic effect, a glimmer of light would shine out of the tomb, and then a blinding light would make people cover their eyes as the entire room was lit up. And that light would be just like Eden, like the first sunrise all over again. It would be like a brand-new creation!

As soon as the light dawned, we'd start playing the entire video backward. We would reverse all of those actions—the same images, just in reverse. Bombs would un-explode over cities; bullets would go back into guns; forests would grow back; and families and people would retrace their steps backward until they were whole again. All the tragedies reversed to show that the cross was big enough to make it all come back to the beginning, back to how God wanted it to be again, until we were back in Eden, back to a new creation.

We sat there in the meeting, breathless, staring up at all of the ideas on the whiteboard, at our masterpiece. "It's what Sam Gamgee said to Gandalf," one of our media staff said in a *Lord of the Rings* reference. "Is everything sad going to come untrue?"[10]

There was just one little problem. Sometimes things that are so beautiful on the whiteboard, so deep and meaningful as an idea, really don't work in reality.

The evening of Good Friday came, and our family festival and extravaganza was going on outside with thousands of people in attendance. They had their fish fry. Their bounce houses. They pet the donkey in the petting zoo. And then they all came into the building for the big worship service to focus on the meaning of the cross. And as they walked in, eyes still adjusting from the bright daylight outside, what did they see on a huge screen? Famine. Pestilence. Concentration camps. The Hindenburg going up in flames. Hitler coming and marching to power. Bombs falling.

Children whimpered and asked their parents what was going on. Elderly people were squinting and whispering to each other. Even when it all ran backward, the initial gloom and doom had already had such an impact that it was hard for that one little moment, the light at the end, to really have an impact. Let's just say it wasn't the cheeriest start to a worship service ever. We got calls and emails from the congregation about that one for quite a while.

That's not so far from how it really works though. We know that ever since the first Easter, God has been running the clock backward, using the power of the cross, the power of the empty tomb, to reverse all the curses that have run rampant in the creation he calls "very good." But you and I are still caught somewhere in the middle, watching it unfold. Even though we're on the victory side of history, we are still stuck in the footage.

Joy to the World

I remember in elementary school when we still watched "films" in class. Usually on Fridays (when the teacher was worn-out and tired of trying to keep our attention), she would declare it was "educational movie time" and pull down the screen at the front of the class. We still used an actual projector wheeled in from the library, with an actual reel of black film that ran from a full circle onto an empty circle while we watched, heads down in the darkness, trying not to fall asleep. At the end it all had to be rewound. Literally, re-wound onto the original spool. The teacher would push a button, and we'd get to watch it in a rapid rewind that sent all the black shiny film back to its original position. One time, the teacher pushed that button and left the room, and something went wrong. I don't know if the empty spool was stuck or if something got jammed, but the full reel started running and spit the film out onto the floor. The whole classroom of kids watched in fascination (and horror that maybe we would get blamed when the teacher returned!) as a shiny black pile of chaos pooled into a snaking heap on the floor. The teacher's face when she walked back in the room was horror-struck and accusatory. We hadn't done anything to cause the situation. We just watched the story unspool into chaos on the floor. Our teacher dashed off for the librarian—keeper of the films as well as books in those days—who quickly brought the next reel so she could gather this one in her arms and take it back to the library to be slowly wound back into place.

This is what it felt like to watch a virus scattering sickness and mayhem that would spread largely unchecked around the world, as if the story God had made was unspooling before our eyes. Bodies suffered. Economies crashed. Schools emptied. Relationships stood at a distance without hugs or gatherings, without celebrations or funerals, all of our points of connection at a standstill while we waited for someone to push rewind.

The Christmas carol "Joy to the World" has always held a hidden spot in redemption history for me. In the middle of all the other carols waxing nostalgic about a sleeping baby and his glowing parents, with lowing cattle looking on, this one cuts right through chaos's heart.

> *No more let sin and sorrow grow*
> *nor thorns infest the ground;*
> *he comes to make his blessings flow*
> *far as the curse is found.*[11]

"Far as the curse is found," the Christmas carol tells us. How far has the virus of sin traveled? As far as human impact has covered the earth. Even in the places unseen by human eyes and on the ground yet untouched by human feet, our impact is felt. But as far as any curse has reached, Jesus' cure will go farther, uprooting sin and death and sickness and tears, upturned pots of soil that kids have upended on the living room rug and terrorists who would threaten and kidnap their mom if given a chance. "What the hell!" the world asks as they look on, watching chaos's unflattened curve. But you're looking in the wrong direction, we answer. That's the promise of the cross: the film runs backward. All that is sad will come untrue. Joy to the world indeed.

PART 2

Effects

Chapter 4

THE MESS IN
THE MAKING

Piles of fabric scraps spill over a quilter's table. Dirty dishes and sticky butter wrappers obscure the counters of a kitchen where little clouds of flour drift in the air. A writer's desk sits in a total shamble of disorder—scribbled notes surrounding towers of books precariously stacked into a compost heap of ideas. Disaster zone or work in progress, who can tell?

The making of things is a messy business. Peek into a kitchen in the middle of a recipe or step into an artist's studio as a painting blooms out of the canvas. It's likely that the first thing you notice won't be the work in progress itself, but the mess that all the creating has created.

If you've ever plunged your hands into raw meat loaf, mixing it in a bowl before its appointment with the oven, you know how hard it is to imagine the appetizing feast just an hour or so away. Raw ingredients are pure potential, full of promise, but not yet fit for consumption. This is also the case for raw ideas and raw vision still in the minds of those who do the creating. Think twice before asking an artist, "What is it you're working on?" You may find yourself in the path of an unprocessed stream of thoughts that flow forth. Words can't really do justice to a masterpiece in the making, and trying to process their muddled, half-baked state could give anyone a stomachache.

Artists have a notorious reputation for being a bit chaotic themselves. Describe someone as having an "artistic temperament," and you aren't exactly describing them as the steady, dependable type you'd ask to cosign on a loan. The stereotype of the scattered creative or the tortured artist brings to mind a person filled with inner extremes that may drive them to distraction, depression, or emotional extremes. Do we have to be falling apart on the inside to put beautiful things together on the outside? Is it true that only those who suffer can create?

In truth, there are plenty of meticulously organized and mentally fit creatives. There are also just as many absent-minded professors, executives, and scientists. A journalist who heard the news that Einstein had just died rushed to the scientific genius's office to capture the state of his work his last day on earth. The surviving photograph shows a desk hidden under crumpled, disorganized papers and a bookshelf half-filled with books stuffed in sideways. This, from the man who gave us the intricate yet simple formulas that explain the nature of our universe. Messy genius, it seems, isn't limited to the arts.

Then there is the great debate about whether a messy environment helps or hurts the creative process. For some, working in a cluttered space throws them off-balance, keeps them from collecting their thoughts and ideas. For others, the messier the room, the more fertile the mind. From somewhere under their compost of clutter their best work rises from a place no one else can see. Whether you prefer a pristine work area or a chaotic one, there's no question that whatever you're making, you're likely to make a mess along the way. This is the reason for erasers, drop cloths, and drafts. It's also why kitchens have sinks.

Psychologist Kathleen Vohs set out to research the question of how a messy environment might impact creativity and innovation. She and her team organized two separate rooms in their laboratory. Or rather, they organized one and disorganized the other, with untidy, cluttered spaces and papers strewn about. They found that their subjects surrounded by chaos made choices that were more innovative and more creative when it came to problem-solving and brainstorming. It turned out that being subjected to the disruption of chaos can loosen up our ordered minds, shaking them out of their ruts to become open to novelty and originality.[12]

While many embrace the proverb "cleanliness is next to godliness," it seems that chaos and creativity are next-door neighbors.

A Marriage of Creativity and Chaos

Creating gives us a chance to gather scattered thoughts and pull them into orbit, bringing them into focus from the theoretical to the tangible. Ideas that were once hidden on the outskirts of our minds are formed into words, notes, canvas, clay. These are places where others can now witness what the creative before only felt inside. Their dreams have become actualized and shared. This is a hopeful and terrifying realization: *Huzzah! Others will look on what I have made. Oh no! Others will look on what I have made.*

Creativity is not foremost an act that one does with the hands. It begins deep in a hidden place inside the one creating. Before something forms in our hands, it exists first in the rough landscape of the mind. The hidden seed of this creation is a rough nugget, a lump turning inside the rock tumbler of the mind against sand and grit, bumping rough edges with ideas and experiences in the jumbled and messy landscape of the mind.

The creative storehouse is less a museum of beautiful ideas than it is a junk drawer. Creatives spend their lives collecting the world into impressions. Noticing. Watching. Listening. If you see someone daydreaming, staring off into space, they could be distracted or bored, but they may be creating, absorbing and processing the things around them, dropping them into the drawer, and listening to how they ring against their surroundings. Part of the mess in the making isn't on the cluttered desk or scratched-out notations of the musical staff, but inside the creative themselves. Ideas and materials turning, rumbling up against each other like a rock tumbler polishing them until they're ready to come forth.

A little boutique opened recently near our home to sell items handcrafted by local artists. Macramé wall hangings drape the rough brick walls above shelves packed with hand-dipped candles, pottery, embroidered baseball caps, and bookmarks painted with scenes of our tiny town. To get to the wooden hoop earrings you must step around a plant cart overflowing with trailing ivy and sprouting succulents. A sign near the entrance proclaims, "Meet Our New Makers!" That's how the owner refers to the people who make and sell things in her shop: makers. Not artists or vendors or creators. Makers. I like the word. It levels the playing field a bit. If I have a hard time seeing myself as an "artist" or a "creative," perhaps I can see myself as a maker.

Maybe you don't identify as a creative person. Can't even draw a stick figure or make an omelet. But because we live in a vast world of raw material, we are all making something of it, all the time. Andy Crouch says that culture is what we make of the world.[13] If this is the case, then we are all makers, the world we're living in layered and re-created gradually by each of us every day, a masterpiece always in the making but never fully made. Creativity is not just for creatives. It takes all of us together to make the world what it is. To take turns mixing ingredients in the bowl of what will be.

When asking someone's opinion, we sometimes inquire, "What do you make of that?" as if by simply expressing judgment you have created something entirely new. Opinions, of course, are a messy medium themselves. When you're having brunch, eavesdrop on the next table, and you'll hear someone talking about the mess the world is in, apparently a worse mess than any we've seen before. But lean toward the table on the other side, and you might catch a story of hope or healing so sweet you find your own faith in the world restored. Are these brunchers living on different planets? Or could the world be its own messy art studio, the splattered drop cloth so intermingled with the work of art itself that it's hard to tell what will emerge as the finished product? Some of us will focus on the mess, others on the masterpiece—even if we're looking on the same scene.

Using the Ingredients at Hand

Since only God creates something from nothing, the rest of us are forced to use the resources that lie in front of us. Our raw materials include not only the good creation that God handed us in the beginning but also the tarnished elements of the fallen world that we live in, touched by sin and tinged with imperfection. Our task at times looks like spinning straw into gold—uncovering glimmers of the original creation to weave into what we make of the world. Other times, we are the ones who end up unweaving the tapestry, spinning the gold back into straw—makers of mistakes, wrong opinions, injustices, and hurts.

What we make, we make with the resources God gave us, mixed with the results of humanity's own mistakes. Our raw materials are both glimmers of heaven and products of hell, weaving life into being with one hand and unraveling it with the other. In our less-than-ideal world, we've been handed a mix of ingredients that have all the beauty of Genesis 1 and all the catastrophe of Genesis 3. Here is the world. What will you make of it?

None of us make it in life using only the easy ingredients. Picture one of those cooking shows where they give you a nice basket of ingredients and you begin making beautiful, tasty plans for . . . what? A key lime pie? A chocolate torte? And then, *Boom!* Halfway through the recipe, they throw in a secret surprise ingredient. Sardines! Put *that* in your cake! Plot twist.

Many of us have experienced the same thing as we sort out the ingredients we're handed in life. We read the recipe carefully, slowly combining what we think will work best, when all of a sudden, a new ingredient appears. A child with learning challenges. A career that never takes off the way we dreamed. A parent with dementia. Plot twist! How will it all come out of the oven now?

We're all making something of the basket we've been handed. Making decisions. Making opinions. Making mistakes. Whether you can carry a tune or draw a self-portrait, you're one of the artists now, which is to say, one of this earth's population. The question is no longer, "Are you a maker?" but, "What do you make of it all?" We are all making something of ourselves as we make this chaotic and messy world into something to live in together. Consider the end of your day as compared to the beginning. What is in the world at dusk that was not there at dawn? A meal well prepared and enjoyed? A conversation? A compliment? A freshly mown lawn or a reassuring smile? All of these are creations. Less straw. More gold.

Let It Happen

The idea that creating is chaotic work came as no surprise to me. There was a time when trying to make a baby was making a mess out of me. With all the trouble we had getting pregnant, it just seemed unfair that I'd have trouble staying pregnant too. But despite the doctor's attempt at reassuring us that many first pregnancies end in loss and that things would be different the next time, they weren't. An unfortunate pattern emerged. When we'd finally come up with a positive pregnancy test, we'd be elated. But before we were even brave enough to share the news with friends, our hopes would be dashed by miscarriage.

Occasionally when a well-meaning friend or family member would ask about our plans to start a family, I'd make some small reference, a dip in the ocean that was our relentless grief, that would let them know we were struggling. "Oh, well, at least you can have fun trying," one responded brightly. Anyone who has journeyed through infertility knows how quickly the fun or spontaneity and even the sex is taken out of the equation. I once joked that when we did have children and they were old enough to wonder where babies came from, I would say: "You see, sweetie, when a mommy and daddy love each other very much, they go to suite 203A of the medical building, fill out some paperwork, and put on a paper gown . . ." For the next few years, there were a lot of waiting rooms, mountains of paperwork, a landfill full of flimsy paper gowns.

Eventually we found ourselves back on the roller coaster again, with a brand-new plus sign in hand and a new specialist with a higher level of expertise in making pregnancies stick, complete with a new stack of bills that came at a higher level as well. We sat down in an opulent high-rise waiting room funded by the money of tearful parent wannabes like us and looked around at the other couples staring back at us, all of us wondering which ones among us would get their happy ending.

After an initial medical history, I left Jim in the exam room and headed off to the bathroom to give a urine sample and put on the much softer cotton gown our upgrade afforded us.

I came back from the bathroom in tears, shaking my head and telling Jim we might as well leave and save our money. There were traces of bleeding, small signs I knew all too well as the beginning of the end. Again. The doctor walked in, and I felt again like a fraud, a not really pregnant woman, there under false pretenses. Who needs an expensive high-risk pregnancy doc when the pregnancy itself wasn't even going to take root? "Let's just take a look," the doctor said, and she asked me to "hop up" on an exam table. (Why did they all tell you to "hop"? Was that something they taught them in medical school?)

The lights dimmed, and we looked over at the little screen that had broken our hearts so many times before. But instead of emptiness, there it was—a tiny blinking light. A heartbeat, complete with a whooshing, rhythmic soundtrack we could hear over the tinny speakers. Not another ending, but a beginning.

We walked out into the bright world an hour later, stunned and clutching the ultrasound printout with a picture of our tiny blinking light, rehearsing the detailed protocol we had been given: a series of prescriptions, multiple daily injections, and a plan for a weekly return visit to monitor the little miracle inside. This rhythm of weekly appointments, twice-daily shots, and constant reassurance of the baby's status kept me busy and focused on the goal. If I could see the light blinking on the screen, slowly growing into the shape of a human, then it must be true. I held my breath each and every time we peered into the dark screen, feeling the cumulative weight of all the bad news I had been given in that posture, but hopeful that our stream of good news would continue.

Then came the appointment when my doctor broke up with me. "You were high-risk for early pregnancy, but we have no reason to think things won't go smoothly from here on out. I'm taking you off all meds and sending you back to your regular doc, who won't need to see you more than the usual monthly visit. Congratulations! You've graduated. Don't come back here again!"

She was grinning as if she'd just given me some really good news, but all I could think about was no more daily shots to be sure we were doing something to keep the baby alive, no more weekly visits to see if the little heartbeat was still flickering. The bruising shots, the side effects, even the driving to an appointment in downtown traffic once a week had all been welcome signs that the baby was alive and well and worth fighting for. I stared at her as if she'd just snatched away my security blanket. "But if I'm not doing all those things to make sure this pregnancy continues, what am I supposed to do?" I asked. "Just let it happen," she said as she patted my shoulder lightly and ushered me to the checkout desk.

Let it happen? Those were short, simple words, but somehow I couldn't understand what they meant. Up to that point, my experience trying to get pregnant and stay pregnant had all been things I *made* happen, not things I *let* happen. Even when the prescribed actions were painful, stressful, or left me with side effects, at least I was doing something.

The fact that I was joining the ranks of "normal pregnant women" was somehow the opposite of comforting. I was facing the fact that all expectant moms face at one time or another: that something was going on inside me, at my very core, that was totally beyond my control. I could no more manipulate the growing limbs and organs or add to the proteins being built into vital structures and systems than I could move the planets in space. Every woman who carries a child faces the fact that she is a vehicle commandeered, steered out of her lane, by an unseen driver that changes everything. The outcome could be her fondest dream or her worst nightmare, but she is not in charge of it. "Let it happen" had never been part of my vocabulary before, and I didn't like it one bit.

I was taken from a world where my anxiety was alleviated by my own actions. Now, told to do nothing at all, I worried about the opposite guarantee: if my actions were producing the outcome I desired, my inaction would produce the outcome I most feared. "Let it happen" was easier heard than done. If I wasn't in control, then who was? Something besides a baby needed to grow in me during that season. It was no wonder that so many of the promises in Scripture seemed so passive: "Let the peace of Christ rule in your hearts" (Colossians 3:15). Or even the response of another scared pregnant woman: "Let it be done to me according to your word" (Luke 1:38 TLV). When the outcome we desire is out of our hands, we are reminded that waiting on God is our greatest hope. The message is obvious: you are not in charge here. Where hope is concerned, you are simply the incubator.

Creating, it turns out, has always been a pattern of action and reflection. Doing and being. Rushing and resting. It may sometimes look like computer keys flying, paint splattering, jumbled ingredients whirring away in a mixer. But creation in process can also look like nothing is happening at all—dough rising, baby gestating, seeds planted and packed firmly beneath the dark soil. Sometimes there's nothing to do but wait. Listen. Watch to see what sprouts from the depths. Let it happen.

The Chaos of Waiting

When you sit down to create something, you can't help but face the chaos of the hard work before you. There's the obvious mess on the workbench (whether your bench is a screen or a countertop or the seed of a company being built), but there's also the chaos of the waiting. The chaos of dreaming up ideas that absolutely will never work. The chaos of letting things happen gradually and in their own time when you are the sort of person for whom a Nike ad is a better mantra. "Just do it" provides so much more direction than "Let it happen."

Creative work is chaotic. It's something new bursting forth and wreaking havoc on the world around it, making a glorious mess of the kitchen and leaving a sink full of dishes in its wake. But it's also the watchful eye of a gardener who has said goodbye and "until we meet again" to the seed. That watchful time is just as generative, just as fruitful, after the work has gone underground.

When the action phase of the work returns, it can be sudden and unbidden. Ideas pop into your head, marinated and ready to go, at the most unusual times. Aha! Eureka! The epiphany moment. Those who study the creative process have coined this as the bed/bath/bus moment, named for some of the common places where unbidden ideas emerge. Sometimes if you turn away from the chaos of work long enough, your brain will continue on without you. Your subconscious mind may produce the answer to a question that no amount of working on scratch paper could solve. This is true of mathematical proofs and problem-solving, but it can also occur in creative work. Sometimes after you've been feverishly at work creating and you turn aside to the mundane, without warning, while you're lying in bed/standing in the shower/ riding in the car somewhere, it hits you. As if by magic.

Once when I was a child, my mom and I started a craft project—a latch hook rug where the image of an owl emerged as we tied yarn in decorative knots. When our initial enthusiasm waned, we stuffed the mess of yarn back into the box and shoved it in a cabinet, where it lay forgotten for over a year. When we discovered the project later, both of us had forgotten how it worked. The directions lost, we put the box aside. Then one night in a dream, I looked down and found my hands holding a little silver hook, wrapping yarn counterclockwise, and securing it to the rug as a pattern emerged. It was almost like watching an instructional video, only I was the one doing the instructing.

Some part of me knew and remembered how to work that tiny little hook. But the part of my brain that stored the answer wasn't about to give it up while I was puzzling hard to come up with the solution myself. The memory had to rise like bread dough, revealing itself only when I let it rest.

The truth is that we give far too much credit to our active minds. The idea that we make our work happen solely by some effort of our consciousness may be an illusion or, at best, an overstatement. Something deep within takes the wheel when we aren't trying too hard. Sometimes we get in our own way, and it's only after we step away from the work that we are able to do something about it.

When we struggle to move forward in producing, creating, or solving, we tend to describe it in negative ways: writer's block, or not being able to "get in the zone." Artists, scientists, and researchers describe reaching points in their work when they can't move forward, and they find themselves searching for creative solutions but encountering roadblocks and problems instead. What if all these blocks, pauses, and hindrances aren't glitches or mistakes in the system? What if they're part of the system itself? A system with cycles of action and reflection built in, where every so often our brain comes to a place where it pauses intentionally and collects itself before proceeding to even greater work. That period of frustrating, humbling pause reminds us that every element of our creative work is a gift. Sometimes we just have to wait to receive it.

Hatching a Miracle from Chaos

It's the very first week on earth. God's paintbrushes are still damp from the intricate landscapes he has just unfurled.

The wet clay of creatures he has designed and set in motion is still setting. He has created, observed, and taken pleasure in his work, repeating over all he has made, in a cadence of enjoyment after each day—good, good, good, and, at the last stroke, *very* good. Then instead of an encore, instead of a thundering repeat of productivity, he pauses. On the seventh day, God rests. The point of the productivity, it turns out, is to enjoy it.

Our church once produced a little coloring booklet for kids about creation that was six pages long. On each of the six pages was the element God made on that day that they could color and learn more about, reflecting on God's good work in seas and skies, birds and fish, and human families. But as I turned to the end, I wondered, *Where is the seventh page?* Without a Sabbath we are trapped in an endless cycle of making. The need for the seventh day exists now more than ever, even if it's something we don't know how to draw or color.

The gift God gave on the seventh day wasn't leisure or recovery. It didn't happen because God was tired or out of ideas. God is the epitome of order. His rest is the opposite of chaos. It's not creation's work paused, but instead the enjoyment of chaos under control, creation's work completed. The seventh day isn't a picture of inactivity or disengagement; it's the moment the very Creator of all things moved in as a resident to enjoy creation alongside the inhabitants he made there.

"Come to me, all you who are weary and burdened," Jesus echoes, "and I will give you rest" (Matthew 11:28). Living with Jesus is an invitation to recognize that we are now living in day seven. We can settle in alongside him for a life of action and reflection, enjoying the world he has made, but also seeing it as a place he has invited us to paint with our own brushes as well. Recognizing that we're living now in day seven means we don't have to do all the doing. Because he is here with us, we can let it happen. Too often we only count to six.

Yet on the crowning day, the world holds grandeur and intricacy both too big and too small for us to behold. Back before those seven days, the bowl held chaos and void and darkness, a seemingly hopeless ingredient list if it were not for one thing: the Spirit of God was hovering over the waters. Hovering is one of those words that helps us understand action and reflection. It holds the sense that something amazing is just about to happen, but maybe not yet. To know the hovering Spirit of God is to have hope in this muddled world that converting chaos is possible, that the pain and mess we see today is redeemable.

The word translated "hovering" is a unique word in Hebrew. It's a word of winged nurture, a verb that calls to mind a bird hovering over her eggs, protecting them. The same word in Deuteronomy pictures God caring for us "like an eagle that stirs up its nest and hovers over its young" (Deuteronomy 32:11).

The Holy Spirit will show up hovering over waters again and again in Scripture. The hovering Spirit will always be a sign that chaos is about to be converted, that creation is breaking forth from darkness to newness of life. The Spirit is sent out as a dove over the waters after Noah's flood. The Spirit hovers as a dove descending on Jesus as he comes out of the water of baptism. Each time, it's a mark that creation is beginning all over again.

To know that the Spirit was there hovering at the beginning, converting chaos into creation, is to know that the chaos we live in today is redeemable. I go back to that image again and again when things are hard. It gives me hope that when I see brokenness, when the cracks are emerging in the fabric of the world around me, it's possible that instead of something breaking, something is hatching.

Ancient Christians who worshiped in the language of Syriac took the word for hovering and borrowed it for their liturgy in worship. In Syriac, the verb *hovering*, the one used for the Holy Spirit in Genesis, is used to describe the action of birds who are brooding over their nests, incubating the eggs that will hatch into their offspring. They brought this rare word into their liturgy in two places, using it to call to mind what God was doing not just in the beginning but in their worship services that day.

The first place where they borrowed the imagery of hovering was at the Communion table, where the priest held a hand over the cup in an act of consecrating the wine for the Eucharist. The other place was when they hovered hands over the head of a new bishop being consecrated to lead the church, what we would call the laying on of hands to bless someone for the act of ministry.

Both of these acts are bold imitations of God's actions in creation.

When the hand is held over the cup, it's during a prayer we call the *epiclesis*, the prayer that invites the Holy Spirit to transform the bread and wine on the table in an act of mystery we do not fully understand that takes what is ordinary and makes it extraordinary. In my tradition, we ask God to "make this be for us the body and blood of Christ."

Talk about new creation emerging from chaos! There is no darker, more chaotic moment in history than the cross. For the darkest, emptiest, most chaotic moment of history to be turned into a blessing and celebration for us is just mind-boggling.

To hold up a cup and say that the awful, chaotic moment where Christ's blood was spilled has been transformed into the act that will restore the order of this world is perhaps God's most surprising act of re-creation ever. If God can redeem the evil of the cross, he can redeem any evil situation we face. If he can raise his Son from the dead, then nothing in our own lives is too dead for him to redeem.

When someone hovers their hand in this blessing, they are saying, essentially, "Hatch a miracle from chaos in the cup, Lord."

The second act of liturgical hovering—the hands placed over a bishop at consecration—is a calling down of the Holy Spirit to transform a human heart and bless the person for ministry.

And since we have an understanding of all Christians being called to serve God in the priesthood of all believers, we could say this prayer over each person who follows Jesus: "Here is my heart, Lord. Hover over the chaos there and make it fit for your purposes. Use me to serve you, Lord— even the most broken parts of me."

I'm not sure what's harder: to redeem the chaos against

God himself at the cross or to transform the chaos of the human heart—that's a tough one.

If God can hatch a miracle from the chaos of the cross, we can also dare to ask God, "Lord, hatch a miracle from the chaos in me."

A few months after my high-risk pregnancy doctor dismissed me and left me holding only the instructions to "let it happen," it did. It happened. I lay in a hospital bed, gazing into the face of my son and marveled that all the pain and chaos and loss had come to this—a tiny and beautiful human being whose messy and wonderful life had just begun. I thought about all the parents I'd heard over the years who expressed the wish that they could control their children's actions and outcomes, whether as babies or toddlers or far into adulthood. This was a lesson I figured we had learned early, but we'd need reminders often enough. This life was ours to hold and guide, but in the end, it was not ours at all.

Working in concert with a creative God means being both producer and product, co-creator and created one. We are a mess in the making, but we are also making the mess of the world into something beautiful. Next time the world seems to tear at the seams, or life feels like it's showing cracks under the strain, watch carefully. The cracks where brokenness once grew may turn out to be the exact spot where beauty will hatch.

Chapter 5

HEART PROBLEMS

My friend Cindy was born with a heart murmur, a misfiring aortic valve that left one of the chambers of her heart marching to its own little syncopated drum. Most hearts have four chambers that beat in perfectly synchronized percussion, but hers danced a waltz where there should have been a tango. For heart function, it turns out, three out of four just doesn't cut it. It's not a majority vote.

Pediatric cardiology wasn't a particularly well-developed specialty yet when Cindy was born in the 1950s, and her doctors were hesitant to cut open the chests of babies and tinker with their tiny plumbing unless there were immediate life-and-death consequences. Luckily for Cindy, the best option in her case was a waiting game. Her off-beat heart would support the movement of a baby, a toddler, probably even a child. But at some point, it wouldn't be enough. The trick was finding the right intersection of growth. The plan was for her to wait until her body grew mature enough, her health grew bad enough, and the growing body of medical science grew advanced enough to mean that surgery was finally a good idea.

When Cindy was a young adult, she began to struggle to catch her breath, getting winded easily during activities where she was previously fine. Her doctors checked and found the struggling valve had calcified, making it harder and harder for her heart to keep up. They finally felt confident that their skills and technology were a match to fix her limping heart. And so they did.

A team of surgeons opened her chest, found the problem valve, and replaced it with a mechanical one. And behold, a cardiac symphony commenced, beating in perfect rhythm for the first time in her life. A little mechanical door opened to let blood flow through and then closed (as her human one should have done) to stop the blood from flowing backward. The opening and closing made a little "click," and after her recovery, her kids could put an ear to her chest and hear the ticking of her heart as if she had swallowed a clock like the crocodile had done in Peter Pan's adventure stories.

Open-heart surgery is not something people sign up for unless it's a life-and-death decision. Whether we admit it or not, that's how most of us approach God's work in our lives. Letting God tinker with the parts of life that we're used to running on our own isn't exactly an inviting prospect, even if we've begun to realize that things aren't going so well. Because of that, chaos is sometimes a gift.

When life's monitors go off, alarms beeping, indicating that some piece of us is not firing on all cylinders, it may be the only thing that will make us admit that trying to fix ourselves is only making it worse. Counselors call it "the presenting issue"—the thing that finally brings us in for treatment. The thing that bothers us enough to ask for help is often just a clue to deeper needs we didn't even know we had. That gift of chaos is what helps us surrender, lay our needs on the altar or the operating table, and trust our hearts to the Master Surgeon.

The Insufficiency of a Divided Heart

The heart is the king of Christian metaphors. King David was described as a "man after [God's] own heart" (Acts 13:22), and when David sinned, he asked God to "create in [him] a pure heart" (Psalm 51:10). People who are stubborn and self-serving like Pharaoh are described as those who "hardened their hearts" to God (Exodus 9:34).

The Bible offers heart wisdom such as this: "Where your treasure is, there your heart will be also" (Matthew 6:21); "Rend your heart and not your garments" (Joel 2:13); and "Above all else, guard your heart, for everything you do flows from it" (Proverbs 4:23).

When I was nine years old, I attended a Christian summer camp where we were told, "You can ask Jesus into your heart." Even at nine, I could imagine Jesus moving in where my most vital and intimate of organs beat out the pattern of life itself. I wanted that kind of intimacy with Jesus more than anything, so I breathed a little yes during a prayer, and Jesus moved in.

Over the years, I've learned more nuanced and academic language for the ways God works, but when it comes to talking to Jesus, who has been with me now for almost four decades, I still think about him with the same childlike tenderness as being as close as the beat of my heart.

When I "asked Jesus into my heart" as a nine-year-old, I had no idea how my heart would grow. Whole chambers would be added to store up new interests, dreams, and desires for which I had no vocabulary back at summer camp the day of my first real prayer. New growth meant new areas of devotion.

I was devoted to my interests, my relationships, my dreams for the future. Sometimes I remembered to let Jesus be in charge of those spaces. But some of them were dedicated to shining a spotlight on myself and the image I wanted to project to others. I looked to achievements and approval to reassure me of my worth and value—and boy, did it work! I could fly for a week on a compliment or an accomplishment. But as with all false gods, they burned me with their inconsistencies. I'd find myself constantly worried that people were unhappy with me. None of my achievements seemed enough.

I was still on the Jesus bandwagon, practicing my faith and devotion to God, but with the added devotion to myself setting up shop in the next chamber over. Eventually, I began to notice a sense of spiritual exhaustion, my faith weak where it should have been strong. I'd find my faith growing paler and lacking enthusiasm as those areas of my heart beat out of sync with the part Jesus occupied. I confess that at times I focused my doubt on God, thinking there was something wrong with him rather than wondering if there was something wrong with me.

We can limp along on the beats of the divided heart for a while, but as we mature, the partial devotion won't be enough. As we grow, we need *more* strength, not less. We face growing temptations that weren't there before. The call to put others first clashes with the self that demands to be first in all things. We begin to lead, not just follow, and those roles and responsibilities require spiritual heavy lifting. For a baby Christian, a little heart murmur is distracting but not fatal, but as we grow in faith and years, the divided heart just isn't enough to support us.

The temptation to try to muscle through on our own fading strength is a powerful one. We've limped along up to this point; we can keep it up. But the effort becomes more and more exhausting. Cindy's body outgrew her limping heartbeat. Our spiritual exhaustion or apathy, burnout or dark night of the soul, can show us just how hard we've been trying to do it ourselves. But where heart surgery is concerned, do-it-yourself is never a good choice, especially when the creator of the heart is also the surgeon who longs for us to place it in his capable care. Usually it takes a crisis for us to finally give up and put it there.

Internal Chaos

Psalm 86 is the song of someone facing chaos in their life. This is a poem-prayer from a heart in deep danger and distress that is crying out to God to save him. The threat is imminent. His enemies, a band of rebels, are breathing down his neck, plotting and moving against him. With his life in danger and his heart full of desperation, he pleads with God for help.

But a strange thing happens as he engages with God and asks for deliverance from this very present and tangible physical threat. The greatest threat, he realizes, is not from those who are chasing him but from a much closer source.

> Teach me your way, LORD,
>   that I may rely on your faithfulness;
>   give me an undivided heart,

that I may fear your name.
I will praise you, Lord my God, *with all my heart*;
I will glorify your name forever.

Psalm 86:11–12, italics added

The greatest danger he faces, and thus the central cry of his prayer, is not an external mob of enemies. To put it in the language of horror movies, *the call is coming from inside the house.* As the psalmist realizes that the location of his true struggle is on the inside, the focus of his prayer shifts from external chaos to internal chaos. He begins to beg for a solution to a different kind of problem—a divided heart.

The crisis brought him to God to beg for rescue, but he realizes that if he is not fully God's, how can he dare to ask for God to intervene on his behalf?

To truly encounter God is to have our eyes opened to our own internal struggles. To become aware of God is to become painfully aware of the hidden parts of ourselves. This happens again and again to people like Isaiah ("Woe to me! . . . I am a man of unclean lips" [Isaiah 6:5]) and Peter ("Go away from me, Lord; I am a sinful man!" [Luke 5:8]). It happens in worship services that offer confession as a first step to approaching the Communion table. It happens to us when we think of engaging with God personally but realize we've neglected our relationship with him. Can we even dare to approach him now? What will he think when we come crawling back?

What sends us back is most often the need to solve some problem we cannot fix on our own. Thankfully, those needs are frequent. Almost daily, I find myself crying out, "God,

I need your help with this!" It's the external chaos that makes me desperate, but then the relief of his presence makes me realize all over again that I want to worship him in all my moments, not just the ones when I'm dying for rescue.

Chaos deposits us on God's doorstep over and over again. It's the reason we come, but not the reason we stay. Come for the desperation; stay for the ongoing, life-changing relationship.

When the psalmist goes to God to ask for rescue, his prayer very quickly turns to asking for forgiveness, begging for faithfulness, and longing to worship. He knows he's turning to God because of a problem he needs solved, but he also begins to wish he had been fully focused on God all along. He starts out by asking God to rescue him from the rebels in his life and moves to asking God to rescue him from the rebel in his heart. He needs an undivided heart—and he knows it.

There will always be external chaos. There is no shortage of enemies breathing down our necks. But the greatest threat will always be the enemies we face within. This is the sign of a maturing Christian prayer: a shift from asking God to change the circumstances we face outside to asking him to fix the difficulties we face within, to bring us to the place of unifying our hearts so they beat as one with God's own heart.

Pursuing Silence

I once asked a spiritual director how I could get to a place where my scattered heart would beat for one thing only, and she introduced me to the spiritual practice of silence. Silence was plentiful while I was sitting in her office. I lapped it up like someone dying of thirst. But when I returned home, silence was scarce. There was a noisy toddler in the next room (quiet, as most parents know, can be a suspicious sign) and a phone buzzing with texts and calls from church members. Even if I sat still for a moment, the laundry, dishes, and dust bunnies seemed to shout me down, calling me to get up and tackle the long list of never-ending needs.

"What's the quietest place in your life?" my spiritual director asked me. I thought for a minute. Not my office. Not my bedroom. Not even the bathroom, which those who have small children know is anything but private. I thought about the last time I had experienced real solitude. It was in my car, driving home from work. I had pulled into the garage and sat for a moment to hear the end of the news story on the radio. I turned the car off, but instead of going in, I just sat for a moment. It was the quietest quiet I had heard in a long time, so I just sat still for a few minutes and took deep breaths.

"Okay," she said, "so let's say your car is your cathedral, your monastic cell. Go out to your garage, even if you're not going anywhere, and sit in your car for a while. Just be sure it's turned off."

So I tried it. The car was quiet, but somehow the noise followed me. Not the toddler (being supervised inside the house) or the cell phone (silenced). The noise was in me. The quieter things got on the outside, the noisier things were inside my head. My to-do list followed me, stretching from the immediate to the eternal:

Schedule doctor's appointment.
Take cookies to new neighbors.
Visit all the national parks.
Build memories of charmed but not sheltered
    childhood for kids.
Succeed in life in general.
Get oil changed.

Silence is a good practice for everyone, but it turns out to be an especially essential lesson for those of us who struggle with control, perfection, the illusion that we must fix it all. Instead of a fix that requires us to do something, the treatment is just the opposite kind of to-do list:

Just be silent with God.
Just be silent.
Just be.

This is much harder than it sounds.

I came back and told my spiritual director, "It didn't work. I'm a failure at this silence thing." She laughed and told me that's absolutely what happens to everyone. Then she told me about three different levels of silence. There's silencing the noises on the outside, silencing the noises on the inside, and silencing the will before God.

The first one is probably the easiest, even if you have to hide in your car to find it. But once you get everything quiet outside, everything inside sees its chance to finally get your attention with all the messages you've been drowning out for a while now. That's normal. Simply silence the inner talk and begin again. It may be for just two minutes the first time, but bit by bit the silence will grow.

"The more you practice silence on the outside," she said, "the easier it will be to get to silence on the inside."

"And silence of the will?," I asked.

"That's the whole point," she said. "To be able to sit before God without asking, longing, or needing. Just to be with him."

I wondered when the last time was that I sat with God without a barrage of requests. Prayer time was so hard to come by and the time so short, and I needed to make sure I fit everything in. It was tempting to begin with a few words of praise and get straight to it: "While I have you here, God, there's a long list of things I need you to get busy fixing in the world."

God's will seemed mysterious, unknown, while my will was pretty obvious, especially if you happened to listen in on my prayer time. If God wasn't quick with the answers, I'd be glad to share a few pointers on how to run the world. Instead, as I got comfortable with the uncomfortable levels of silence, I was learning to enjoy the quiet of his presence. To let him know that "your will be done" was enough for me, no matter if it matched my plans or not. This state of surrender wasn't natural to me, but it was the beginning of the "undivided heart" the psalmist sought. Maybe even if the world around me was rippling with chaos, my heart could be a clear and undisturbed pool reflecting God's presence, even if it were to last only a few minutes.

Mixed Emotions or Mixed Motives?

Having an undivided heart doesn't mean we are supposed to be emotional monoliths, frozen ponds whose icy surfaces remain unchanged no matter the circumstances going on around us. It's okay to have mixed feelings and worries that bubble to the surface. The announcement of a friend's success may produce both happiness and a hint of jealousy. The joy of finally finding some time to oneself may come with a twinge of loneliness. Nostalgia is the perfect example of a mixed emotion—where joyful remembrance and grief often meet, all in the span of one memory.

"If I just had enough faith, I wouldn't feel so terrified something bad will happen," a woman pregnant after several devastating miscarriages told me. The guilt she felt was overshadowing the tender shoot of hope that was beginning to emerge. I told her that if she wasn't afraid, I would be worried about her, sure she was either in denial or numbing her valid emotions at the possibility of more loss.

"There's no room for fear and faith," I've heard in dozens of sermons. She had probably heard some of the same ones. But isn't it fear that most often drives us to faith? If we didn't fear anything, what would we need God for anyway?

Hearts are big enough to feel many things at once, and the God who created our hearts is big enough to understand and to sit with us in our confused state. He sits with us in the chaos of unresolved emotions and unknown outcomes.

It's not the mixed emotions that will tear us down, but the mixed motives. The trouble is, these motives are often so faint that they can live undetected beneath the surface until a collision of multiple loves drives them into the light. When we peer into the wreckage, what we often find is the hidden motive to elevate ourselves, the secret desire to acquire power or pleasure or possession that we didn't even realize was the driving force behind our actions. We may not even realize the internal dialogue that is silently pushing us to compare ourselves to others or exaggerate our qualities to make a good impression, measuring up to some unseen standard we wouldn't even recognize. Mixed motives can travel side by side on parallel tracks, picking up speed for quite some time before they are revealed, but the longer they coexist under the surface, the bigger the crash will be when they meet.

I remember one year in particular when the news was littered with stories of well-known leaders whose lives and ministries came crashing down because of years of hidden sexual misconduct. These were names we had followed for years, authors of books we had read, leaders of ministries we had trusted. The chaos in the Christian community had responses bouncing between "burn all of their books" and "they're only human; we all make mistakes." A preacher who came to speak to students at the seminary where I work admonished our community in a sermon on resisting temptation. His great conclusion was to warn the students, "Just keep your zipper up."

This seemed to be good advice in light of the very public chaos raining down that year on the churches and families of leaders whose moments of passion left decades of pain in their wake. "Keep your zipper up" was a good rule for the future leaders sitting in that room, those whose spiritual leadership would either build or break the lives of so many, not just in their own families but in growing circles of influence in churches and ministries.

But reflecting on where the pain and brokenness started, I wondered if the advice had gone far enough. Even a closed zipper wouldn't prevent affairs of the heart, which is where affairs in the sheets begin. It wouldn't stop the sexual harassment of coworkers or the second or third sidelong glance of attraction in a church business meeting. There were no zippers on computer keyboards, where the click of a mouse can take the heart on a damaging journey of secret shame. Depth of character in leadership, humility and respect in interactions—these are found deep in the undivided heart, not in any outward accessory.

A zipper is an outward sign of fidelity, but the heart can cheat without breaking that boundary. If the zipper is the only sign of fidelity that we must follow, the heart will find other ways.

Jesus was making this point before zippers were invented: "You have heard that it was said, 'You shall not commit adultery.' But I tell you that anyone who looks at a woman lustfully has already committed adultery with her in his heart" (Matthew 5:27–28). Jesus knew the heart could conceal all manner of chaos for a time.

A friend once told me that when he said "I do" in his marriage vows to his wife, he was also saying a thousand "I don'ts." To say "I do" to one person is to cancel out the possibility of what we may "do" with any other. This involves far more than just activities involving zippers. The biggest "I don't" that we say in those vows is to ourselves. When we promise to love the other person with all that we are, we are saying we no longer put ourselves first in all things. We will need to sacrifice self for their well-being, to eat at restaurants we don't prefer, to visit in-laws when we'd rather be at the ballpark or the beach, to clean messes we didn't make, and make life choices that put their best interests before our own.

That vow isn't for marriage alone. To fully, wholeheartedly, say "I do" to God is to cancel out the possibility of anything that might compete for the space he wants in our hearts, which is all of it. The hardest "I don't" we say will be to ourselves. "I don't" is a daily answer to oneself when it asks in a thousand different ways, *How about putting yourself and your own needs first today?* The problem is that it's just too easy to answer "I do" to God but keep our fingers crossed, our options open. That little off-beat can trip up a heart, turning a wholehearted symphony into a divided disaster.

The Off-Beat

Tiny signals may pop up to indicate the off-beats of our hearts. We have to listen carefully, leaning in to see if they're beating in or out of rhythm.

I was waiting in a doctor's office with a friend one day when I began to feel restless. My friend was a young, single cancer patient. Our whole community was rallying to take care of her during her chemotherapy treatments, bringing her meals, picking up her groceries, helping her out when she was recovering from a rough treatment. I had the sense that the gold standard of helpers were the people she asked to take her to one of her chemotherapy appointments. Every few weeks, I'd see her post a selfie in the chemo waiting room with a friend in the background and some sweet caption about the people who were really carrying her through the darkest parts of this journey. Finally she had asked me to take her, and here we were, waiting for her appointment.

Strangely, once we arrived, I found myself not entirely focused on what we were talking about. As we waited for her name to be called so she could go back for treatment, a tiny, off-beat distraction kept beating somewhere in me: *I wish she'd go ahead and take the selfie of us and post it so everyone can see that I was here with her.* I was as horrified as if I'd spoken the thoughts out loud.

Did I want to help my friend? Yes. Did I want others to see me helping and think good things about me? Yes. Those two beats pulsed off-kilter with one another in my own heart, a surprise struggle going on where I thought the battle for mastery had been won long ago.

The dual motivations of achievement and approval were still beating somewhere within me, even as I sought to help others. That division was a small one, but ignoring it felt like a dangerous gamble.

David Whyte, a beloved British poet, tells a story about a time he was trying hard to overcome division in his own life. Whyte was early in his pursuit of poetry, his true gift and passion, but he was also working and striving to make a living. He found himself at a dead end in both work and art, tucking poetry in around the edges while he went about trying to live the kind of life he thought was expected of him.

One evening he was meeting with his spiritual director, a monk also named David (Brother David Steindl-Rast), and he blurted out under the pressure of his day, "Brother David, tell me about exhaustion." David Whyte records the conversation that followed, one that would be life-changing for him.

He looked at me with an acute, searching, compassionate ferocity for the briefest of moments, as if trying to sum up the entirety of the situation and without missing a beat, as if he had been waiting all along, to say a life-changing thing to me. He said, in the form both of a question and an assertion: "You know that the antidote to exhaustion is not necessarily rest?" "The antidote to exhaustion is not necessarily rest," I repeated woodenly, as if I might exhaust myself completely before I reached the end of the sentence. "What is it, then?" "The antidote to exhaustion is wholeheartedness."

Brother David went on:

"You are so tired through and through because a good half of what you do here in this organization has nothing to do with your true powers, or the place you have reached in your life. You are only half here, and half here will kill you after a while. You need something to which you can give your full powers. You know what that is; I don't have to tell you."[14]

Whyte talked later about just how pivotal that moment was for him. His exhaustion, he knew, was not just born out of the number of hours he worked or the lack of sleep he was getting. It was an exhaustion that went deeper, all the way to the soul. He was trying to treat poetry, his true love, like a mistress he visited on the side. Brother David's response had diagnosed a dividing wall in his heart, beating so wildly to keep all things together that it was stamping out the fire within him.

The discontent tugging at David Whyte's divided heart was a call to give himself fully to a vocation, to single-mindedly develop his gifts into something that became a gift to the world. Whether we struggle similarly with our calling or our job, we've all experienced areas where we are spiritually exhausted and divided. The words of wisdom he received ring true to us: "You're only half here, and half here will kill you after a while." Following God means giving your whole heart.

It will exhaust us to live with a foot in both worlds, but Jesus knew there was an antidote for those longing for inner unity, for singleness of purpose: "Love the Lord your God with all your heart and with all your soul and with all your mind and with all your strength" (Mark 12:30). Somehow giving all of ourselves in love in all these areas, finding our whole heart beating in the same rhythm for the same things, brings us peace where there has been exhaustion, and clarity where there has been confusion.

Chapter 6

THROUGH THE STORM

When our kids were two and four years old, we left behind our family and friends, church, and neighborhood and moved across the country. I was thrilled when our son Drew came home from preschool one day with his first birthday party invitation. That Saturday, I walked Drew up the front steps of the address printed on the invitation, gift in hand. We had barely knocked when the door swung open and an older woman welcomed us. "I'm Dawn," she said, smiling. "Come on in!"

In the middle of the chaotic scramble of children was the birthday boy, Brody, decked out in a hard hat and beaming from his wheelchair as half a dozen preschoolers orbited around him, chasing balloons in glee. Every once in a while, a balloon would bounce up to Brody's chair, and he'd bat it back, his arm bending jerkily but always finding its target. All of the party games were designed so that Brody could play from his chair. Drew's favorite was a wrecking ball suspended from the ceiling. The kids would build a tower of cardboard blocks and then swing the wrecking ball to see how many they could knock down. Brody's dad, Matt, would set up the blocks for him and then hand him the ball so he could let loose, demolishing the blocks again and again. Brody looked like if he smiled any bigger his face would split.

The party had a construction theme, with a cake covered

in tiny backhoes and bulldozers moving chocolate Oreo crumbs around the little construction site on top.

"This is the first birthday he'll actually get to eat his cake!" Dawn said proudly as she handed me a glass of punch. "His mom, Sabrina, spent all last summer with Brody at a special inpatient therapy place in Pennsylvania where they taught him to eat. The insurance company didn't even want to pay for the therapy. 'He's fine like he is!' they said. 'He can eat through his tube.' But Sabrina fought it, and they finally said they'd cover it if she paid the family's copay up front. Even at a small percentage, their part came to $12,000. Our little town's Walmart had a special family yard sale that raised half of it. They set up a GoFundMe and people from our town paid the other half, and off they went! When they got there, he was getting 100 percent of his nourishment through his feeding tube. Twelve weeks of inpatient therapy—and here's this kid, eating ravenously! Only needs about 15 percent through his feeding tube now. You just watch him take that cake apart!"

Dawn was clearly a very active part of Brody's life. She knew all about his different therapy appointments and the progress he was making. During the party she helped Sabrina, Brody's mom, with all the ins and outs of hosting a crazy gathering full of kids that any young mom desperately needs help with. She had that special smile of pride and ownership that grandmas proudly display at events like these.

At one point I asked her, "I didn't catch whose mother you are—Brody's mom's mom or his dad's?"

"Oh!" she laughed, surprised. "Oh, I'm not his grandma!

I was the labor and delivery nurse in the hospital when Brody was born."

Dawn was there five years earlier when Sabrina went into labor at twenty-six weeks pregnant. She was there when Brody, weighing just one pound, came into the world. She stayed with Sabrina through it all, giving smiles and encouragement and telling her how strong and brave she was. Then Dawn would walk out into the hall and brace herself, taking deep breaths. None of the news was good.

Brody was what they called a micro-preemie. "At just one pound, he wasn't fully developed yet," Sabrina remembers. "He didn't have eyelashes or eyebrows; his ears weren't fully developed yet; and his skin was kind of see-through. He was so beautiful, and he was mine, but it was so terrifying." She loved him with all her heart from that very first second. Sabrina knew God, but they weren't what she would call "close." She didn't have much experience with how God worked, but she knew that when there was a crisis, you prayed. She started praying and didn't stop.

Brody had the deck stacked against him. In his first twenty-four hours of life, he had a stroke, his brain bleeding on both sides. His 20 percent chance of survival dropped to 5 percent. During his first brain surgery, the doctors installed a shunt on each side of his brain, the drains sloping upward out of the top of his skull like he had horns. He was eventually diagnosed with cerebral palsy and hydrocephalus. Sabrina moved into his hospital room and didn't leave. There was no TV, and her pastor had told her that reading her Bible might help, so she just read and read. She read so much that the nurses thought she was crazy. She didn't understand a lot of it, but she kept reading.

They were in the hospital for more than two hundred days in this first year, and 180 days the second. The brain surgeries were so frequent they seemed almost as routine as the milestones other babies hit during those busy months.

When they finally did get to go home, caring for Brody was a full-time job. The state they lived in had very few options for the advanced kinds of therapy Brody needed, so Sabrina was driving him four hours round trip to get an hour of therapy several times a week. Matt traveled for work. Their support system was minimal. They were drowning.

"Some people will tell you that God won't give you more than you can handle," Sabrina says. "That makes me crazy. I can tell you a million times over that God gave me more than I could handle."

The storm she was experiencing was overwhelming. Much more than anyone could handle. Where was the storm-calming Jesus her Bible told her so much about? The one who spoke and changed the chaos into calm?

God on a Cushion

Think about the story of Jesus calming the storm in the Gospels. There's no record of how high the winds or storm surge were, no picture showing the radar or how much rainfall to expect. But even without access to any data about that particular storm, it's clear that it was a terrible one.

Considering that a third of the disciples were seasoned fishermen (Peter and Andrew, James and John—two sets of brothers who have multiple combined lifetimes of experience fishing this exact lake), considering that one of them was probably the owner of the boat they were traveling in, and considering just how scared these burly, grown fishermen were, screaming in terror despite the many storms they must have weathered in their lifetimes, this must have been one powerful squall.

When the storm was at its worst and they were certain they needed help, the disciples went looking for Jesus and found him asleep on a cushion. I love this tiny detail in Mark's gospel—the cushion (Mark 4:38). Even though this story is told in three of the Gospels, Mark is the only one to mention it. The disciples were frantically battening down the hatches and bailing water, and there was Jesus, asleep in the stern, his head nestled on a cushion.

That little detail—the cushion—seems to sum up the disciples' angry reaction to Jesus' seeming disregard for their safety and survival. *If he can sleep while we suffer*, the disciples seem to have thought, *he must not care*. They mistook his slumber for apathy, his calm for callousness.

"Teacher," they said, "don't you even care that we're perishing? Doesn't it bother you just a little that we're about to die while you're catching a few z's? Are you more concerned with your beauty sleep than you are with our lives?"

If we're honest, this is the kind of thing many of us say (or at least think) at one time or another in our lives. When we find ourselves in danger or stress, grief or panic, when we cry out to God and things don't get better (or even get worse), our minds jump to images of God eating bonbons on a cloud somewhere, detached and uninterested while we struggle and suffer and weep.

"My God, my God, why have you forsaken me?" the psalmist asks. "Why are you so far from saving me, so far from my cries of anguish? My God, I cry out by day, but you do not answer, by night, but I find no rest" (Psalm 22:1–2).

You. God on a cushion. Napping while the world suffers. Where were you when I needed you most? Were you asleep on the watch? Do you even care?

In their panic and fear, the disciples have forgotten one little detail about Jesus—his location. He's not far-off or distant or removed. He's in the boat with them—literally in the same boat.

In the middle of a terrifying storm, the disciples were doing what the disciples seem to be so good at—missing the point so that we can get it. God in the same boat is a crystal-clear picture of the incarnation. God has come to earth to walk the same human path we walk, a path that includes splinters and nightmares, suffering and fear. God put himself in the same boat with us and sailed even into the places of our greatest dangers and fears. Jesus will sail this human boat even to the destination of suffering and death. He will hang on a cross and speak the psalmist's words himself: "My God, my God, why have you forsaken me?" (Matthew 27:46). There is no nook of the human experience that he will avoid to preserve his own comfort.

Jesus' presence in the boat with them screams, "I'm right here with you!" even as the disciples scream, "Don't you even care?"

Because Jesus is in the boat, he is close enough, present enough, that the disciples can actually shake him awake. God on a cushion, yes, but a cushion so near that their cries don't even have to travel to heaven to reach his ears. He was right there all the time.

And this God, while unafraid and unperturbed by the storm, stirs when the ones he loves shake his shoulder. It's not chaos that wakes God; it's his loving responses to our needs. He's so utterly unafraid of the things we see as our greatest threats that he can nap right through them. But our concerns reach his ears every time.

Maybe instead of seeing it as insensitive, we might find it impressive that Jesus can sleep through the tempest. It's almost as if Jesus is saying, "Storm, shmorm. I could do this in my sleep." Without breaking a sweat, he turns and banishes the storm with a word. "Peace!" he says. "Peace! Be still!" (Mark 4:39 ESV). I always wondered if these words were meant just as much for the disciples as they were for the storm. Either way, his words calm them both.

Sputtering and gasping, the disciples stare as if they've never seen Jesus before. Once they catch their breath, they turn pale faces to one another and ask, "Who is this? Who is this that even the wind and the waves obey him?" (Mark 4:41, author's paraphrase).

You can almost see the words of the psalm they learned as boys running through their minds: "He stilled the storm to a whisper; the waves of the sea were hushed. They were glad when it grew calm, and he guided them to their desired haven" (Psalm 107:29–30).

"Wait a minute," you can hear them asking. "Wait just

a minute! God is the one who calms the seas. So if the man in the boat has just calmed the sea with a word, just like God does in the Psalms, then *who is this* in the boat with us?" The miracle of the stilled storm pulls back the curtain and reveals the one who speaks chaos into order, emptiness into fullness, light into darkness. The life-threatening storm is gone, and they find themselves face-to-face with the life-giving God. The disciples were certainly paying attention now.

When We Weather the Storm

Many of us start paying attention to Jesus because of a storm. We aren't necessarily looking for God at first; we're just looking for someone who can rescue us out of whatever catastrophe we find ourselves in. We'd like a little dose of what the disciples got on that boat. Waves stilled, winds silenced, stomach-churning circumstances banished.

It would be great if it always worked this way. When Category 5 conditions blow up in your face, just shake Jesus awake like some magic genie and he'll make it all okay. I'd like to sign up for a Christian life that promises a constant crossing from danger to ever safer shores, where we are plucked out of uncomfortable situations and given our own little cushions on which to rest. We'd all get in that boat!

The problem with this image is that we've all seen the forecast. We can tell there are storms that are lasting. I know plenty of people who were living in storms, some of them in Category 5 hurricane conditions, and still were crying out to God to still their storms. What did the God who calmed the storms have to say to my friend Liz, whose brain injury from an accident meant that she lived with her parents, unable to function above the level of a child? What about my friend Steve, whose brilliant wife was slowly disappearing before his eyes because of Alzheimer's disease? Hadn't they called out to the God who calms storms?

If we set God up as the captain who ferries us continually from danger to safety, what do we do with the people who clearly missed that boat?

Years ago, I worked with a young man, sweet and shy, who was the one we all called on when our computers went glitchy or the server went down. He didn't say much in the office beyond "Have you tried rebooting it?" or "Slide over and let me try something." Usually we just saw the back of his head as he walked away once the problems were fixed. But one day he joined a couple of us for lunch, and I happened to mention that I was planning on becoming a pastor someday. That's when he told me he didn't believe in God. After a few halfhearted philosophical arguments for why God couldn't exist, his voice softened and switched to story mode instead. When he was a very little boy, his mom had been diagnosed with cancer. After she had undergone lengthy treatments and exhausting attempts at a cure, his dad sat him down and let him know the doctors couldn't do anything else for her. "It's all in God's hands now," his dad said. In his little-boy mind, this was happy and hopeful news. Surely God's hands were more capable than any doctor's, weren't they? But then his mother died. "That's when I gave up on God," he said. "That was it for me."

I've heard lots of variations on his story. If we're taught that the only thing that happens in "God's hands" is that stormy circumstances cease and all is made right again, we quickly recognize there's an error somewhere in the equation. Like my friend at work, many come to the conclusion that God must not exist at all. But there are other people I've met who are still on the boat, weathering the storm—some of them for years—and they haven't thrown the idea of God's presence overboard yet.

God Moves In

In Genesis 16, we find the story of Hagar—Abraham and Sarah's servant, a woman who was desperate and alone—crying out to God. Even though she was a slave and a foreigner, Hagar is the first person to give God a name in the Bible. It happens when she ran away into the desert, pregnant with her master's son and mistreated by her master's wife, who was jealous of her pregnancy. Desperate, despondent, and near death, Hagar met God in the desert. God rescued her, brought her back home, and promised to bless her and her offspring. "You are the God who sees me," Hagar said, giving God the first of many names humanity would bestow on him: *El Roi*, the God Who Sees. "I have now seen the One who sees me," Hagar marveled (Genesis 16:13).

Of the people who know Hagar's story, many of them forget she went to the desert not once, but twice. The first time she was pregnant and scared and ran there herself.

But after her son Ishmael was born, Abraham and Sarah miraculously conceived a baby in their old age. Now they didn't need Ishmael as an heir, and she and Ishmael were at best a nuisance, at worst a threat to Sarah and Abraham's growing miracle. Sarah kicked Hagar out and sent her back to the desert, this time with her young son in tow. This time there was no home to go home to. This time Hagar was doubly desperate because of the son she loved. Certain they were going to die in the desert, Hagar laid her son under a bush and went "about a bowshot away" to weep and mourn (Genesis 21:16). She just couldn't bear to watch the boy she loved suffer and die.

This time, when God showed up, he wasn't there because he saw; he was there because he heard. And it's not Hagar's cries God was responding to. An angel told Hagar, "Do not be afraid; God has heard the boy crying as he lies there" (Genesis 21:17).

God wanted her to know she was not the only one paying attention, not the only one who cared if her son had a hope and a future. Hagar had been crying out for rescue, but it doesn't say God heard *her*; it says God heard *her son*. God wanted her to hear loudly and clearly that she was not the only one responsible for his life. He wanted her to know that she may be his mother, but that she could never be his God.

Caregivers: Bringing Calm in the Storm

Hagar's story was one that Sabrina read on those long days in the NICU, just a bowshot away from the incubator that held her tiny baby, who had not yet learned to cry. God wanted Hagar to know he was listening to her sweet boy, so she would know she'd never have to carry that burden alone. God whispered the same thing, all those years later, to Sabrina.

None of us are fully responsible for the fate of another person, even if we are responsible for their care. Sometimes we feel like we're bearing someone's burden alone, that without our striving, without our care, someone we love will fall through the cracks. But God hears them. God sees them. And his help will be the thing that gets them (and us) through it all.

Hagar's two trips to the desert both include an encounter with a saving God, but they differ in their endings. The first time Hagar ran to the desert, God brought rescue by bringing her out of the desert and safely returning her home. The second time, God moved in and made a home for Hagar and her son in the desert. Instead of moving them out, God moved in.

Storm or desert—one is a deluge of too much, one the deprivation of too little. Both are chaos. But God is in the storm. God is in the desert. Chaos may be where we live for some time, but we are never alone at that address.

Caregivers live in a special kind of storm, one that does not have a clear and visible end. The words "Peace! Be still!" are theirs in a special way, because they don't still the storm; they still the people in the storm.

Sabrina desperately needed a God who looked down and saw her and her struggles, who picked her up out of the desert and made it all better. Family and friends who had been supportive at first faded into the background as their struggle stretched on. "Brody's struggle is hard for people to watch sometimes," Sabrina says. "So lots of people choose to love him from a distance."

Meanwhile, Dawn stayed in touch. She had recently moved to central Kentucky, to an area none of them had ever heard of. Sabrina struggled to find Brody the support he needed—and to find her own support as well. She remembers breaking down and thinking, *I can't handle it here anymore. Our kid deserves better.* As Sabrina researched places that had the kind of support kids like Brody needed, she discovered that Kentucky was one of the best. When Matt came home that Friday, she told him they were moving.

The new area had a school with "inclusion classrooms," where Brody was placed in a class with other kids his age. A teacher's aide was assigned just to him, who helped him through the day, and he now had a class full of new friends, including my son Drew. Sabrina remembers what a big deal it was for him to be with other kids his age and want to do what they were doing. His progress exploded.

When Sabrina and Matt moved with Brody to central Kentucky, Dawn and her husband were the only people they knew, the closest thing they had to family. Matt began looking for other work, something that wouldn't require him to travel far from home so much. He decided to pursue firefighting, something he had wanted to do since he was a little boy. We lift up firefighters as heroes—frontline workers, we call them—who go to a job every day where they keep people alive by putting themselves in hard places. Caregivers are frontline workers on the most hidden lines of all, showing up every day (and sometimes all night too) to preserve life. Sabrina has a little life depending on her. That life is growing and thriving, learning to communicate and feed himself and play with friends.

Brody's growth is an answered prayer. It also creates new challenges. Sabrina talks about working out so she can continue to lift her growing boy. Matt is a burly six foot three. Brody will likely weigh as much as Sabrina someday. When she thinks back to the tiny, one-pound translucent baby, she smiles. Every one of his fourteen brain surgeries, every ounce of weight on him, is a storm she and Jesus have fought through together.

She knows there are still more storms ahead. God is a caregiver too. He cares for Sabrina and Matt even as they care for Brody. Those who care for the vulnerable are an indispensable part of so many lives, and God has promised never to leave them alone as they weather what must seem like endless storms.

The Creator of the Waves

The only time I've been "at sea" for any length of time was on our honeymoon cruise. The ship was so vast that at times we forgot we were not on dry land. We could dine, dance, sleep, go to the theater—all without any real reminders that we were hundreds of miles from land, out in the middle of the Caribbean. The ship was so large that we rarely felt it moving at all.

One night toward the end of our cruise, I woke to a strange sound inside our cabin—the clinking of metal against metal inside the closet. It was the clothes hangers shifting back and forth on the rod and clanging against each other. We had sailed into a nighttime storm. The boat was pitching back and forth, but in our sleep, we felt none of it. Only the hangers gave it away.

The next morning, I mentioned the storm to one of the staff. "It was a doozy," he said, "but the ship's too large for you to feel much except the biggest waves. Besides, the closer you are to the center of the ship, the less the storm will toss you about."

Knowing the size of that ship and how most of the waves were no match for it, I can't imagine the size of the storm that night as we slept. If we had been in a little boat like the disciples were in on the Sea of Galilee, it would have capsized for sure. But it turned out that what mattered was not the size of the storm but the size of the ship that was carrying us through it. And the closer we were to the center of that ship, the less we felt the storm.

So many people are looking at the prognosis of a life of long-term chaos, of sailing through a very long storm. But here's the thing with Jesus: the closer you are to the center, the less the waves have your attention.

Sabrina says she gets all kinds of reactions from people who meet Brody, now a growing little boy who needs a new wheelchair fitted for him every couple of years. "People say 'I'm sorry' a lot. 'I'm sorry you have to go through so much. I'm sorry Brody isn't like other kids.' I get that from people a lot. I want to say to them, 'I'm sorry, but you don't know our life! Can you see the goodness our life has? There's so much goodness!' In my walk with God, I've worked so hard to see the goodness in all the badness. Yes, our life is different. But it is still good. I can't even put into words how blessed we are to have Brody. Because there was a very dark point in our lives when we just didn't know if he would be here or not. The tough beginning has changed our perspective on all the rest of it.

"I've got this child who is so different, but he is so precious, and it's our job to show him all of the beautiful things in the world and make his life such a better place to be in. It's beautiful, this ugly mess of a life. Brody is the one who showed me that."

Sometimes chaos is a permanent address, an unrelenting place where we find ourselves dodging waves and leaning into the wind without any forecast of clearer skies. But look around, and you find the creator of the waves is right there in the boat with you, a seat he chose on purpose, storm or no storm, because he knew you'd need him there. There's no shame in shaking Jesus awake when you need him. Many of us find Jesus because of a storm of some kind. And when we find him, he's not threatened at all by the things that threaten us. He's so calm that the things that rock us to our core simply rock him to sleep.

The disciples mistook his slumber for indifference, but isn't it good news that Jesus is undisturbed by the things that disturb us? Would we rather he be screaming and white-faced too? Instead what we find is that a God who doesn't consider chaos enough to even lift an eyelid awakens at our cries and speaks peace into our lives. Who is this that, even as the storm rages on, can bring my attention to the beauty in this ugly mess of a life?

The candles were lit on top of the little construction site of a cake, and all the kids gathered around. After they sang, they all puckered up their little lips like they were going to blow out the candles, but then they paused, resisting the urge until Brody could gather enough breath to blow them out for himself. I'll never forget how proudly they cheered for him when he did it. It was quite possibly the most beautiful party I had ever been to.

PART 3

Response

Chapter 7

IN REMEMBRANCE

When our son Drew was a baby, I longed for the day he would learn to talk, to tell me what was going on in his little baby head. I would walk around the house with him sometimes, holding him up and showing him things to encourage his growing communication skills. I'd touch a window and say the word *window* a couple times. Then I'd move on to say *bed* or *light* or *fan*. Each of these I repeated slowly, enunciating carefully in an airy voice.

One day, I walked with Drew into our master bathroom, which was decorated all over with stars. There were stars on the shower curtain, stars on the hand towels, stars on the toothbrush holder.

In the tiny inner room where the toilet sat, a large brass star hung on the wall over the commode. Intending to teach Drew the word, I walked into the tight quarters, balancing the baby on my hip, and reached out and touched the heavy star. I didn't realize that the nail that held it in the drywall was unstable. At my light touch, the nail holding up the star ripped right out of the wall. Before I could say the word, the star fell and hit the metal trash can with a loud boom.

The deafening noise of metal hitting metal rang out, echoing through the tiny room. I glanced quickly to see what effect it had on my infant's sensitive ears, but surprisingly, Drew didn't even whimper. I think we were both in shock. We just stood there staring.

When I finally collected my wits enough to speak, I searched for words my little one could grasp, words that would explain the assault our ears had just taken in. But when I finally opened my mouth, all that came out was, "Uh-oh!"

That was it. "Uh-oh!"

And after a long moment, we moved on.

After *ball* and *duck*, one of Drew's first words was *star*—a fact that made my husband claim he was an early Dallas Cowboys fan. But I knew better. The shape of the bathroom stars had crept into his consciousness—all that pointing at the repeated pattern on the shower curtain had made an impression.

Months later, I was still making the rounds with Drew, touching and naming things in the house. I was beginning to see fruit from the naming game, as Drew began to repeat words back to me. When I carried him into that little room where the heavy brass star hung, I lifted my hand to say *star*, but Drew beat me to it. Before I could speak, his high baby voice rang out in that space. But he didn't say the word I expected. Instead, he said, "Uh-oh!"

Well, that, of course, confirmed my maternal suspicions: my son was a genius! Stephen Hawking with a binkie. Albert Einstein in Pampers. He reached back in memory, made a connection between an object and an event, and found the right word to communicate it. What brilliance!

In reality, I had just witnessed one of those normal milestones of early human development, experienced by every typical child but miraculous to every parent. I had watched as my son made a memory.

When he looked at that space where the star had hung,

it rang a distant bell inside him: *Something happened here.*
The star was no longer just a star; it was a memory of an
uh-oh. I recognized that when we walked through the house
and through life together naming things, we weren't just
sharing a common language; we were making a shared
story. I never knew that such a mundane moment could
thrill my heart so deeply.

How much more must God enjoy watching our experiences form memories! I can picture him gazing with joy
as the same thing happens with us, saying to us, "That's
right. That's it." He is with us as we meet people, go places,
see familiar objects. At some point, instead of just learning
facts or recognizing things, we begin making memories.
Living a common story with God.

The Bible is full of God's declarations that his people
are to infuse the places and objects around them with the
memories of their experiences with God:

Build an altar.
Raise up a stone.
March around these walls.
Shake the dust from your feet.
Take off your shoes . . . this is holy ground.
Do this in remembrance of me.

In God's presence, the places and objects in our lives
become more than what people see. They are infused with
an experience of God. When a memory forms, it forms us.

God must have known that memories would help us
order the chaos of our lives. They gather up what would be

scattered words and experiences and give them not only language but meaning. Memories order our jumbled experiences into pins on a map. They help us connect the dots into stories that overlap our journeys with other travelers. "Remember that time we . . ." Those words are the foundation of community, of family, of a life lived with others instead of fragmented and alone.

The Gift of Shared Memory

Exploring new cities when traveling alone for work has always been one of my favorite adventures. But sometimes on the way home, I ache for someone to turn to and reflect on the best and worst moments. The memories dissolve more quickly when they're only stories we report or pictures we show. "Wish you were here!" we write on vacation postcards. The sentiment is the opposite of "Remember that time we . . ." It dissolves our experiences into anecdotes, a story told instead of a story shared.

The desire to share our journey with someone is even more pronounced when things take a turn toward suffering or loss. If sharing our happy stories helps us organize and reflect on our memories, then the stories infused with chaos are the ones we need to share with someone the most. Remembering the toughest things we've been through demands a witness, someone to remember that we were strong and resilient, that we survived. We need someone who is willing to listen as we recite our memories. Memories in isolation can create a circle of loneliness.

God is an ever-present memory sharer. In fact, he is the only one who will stand as a witness with us in every situation we ever encounter. He is ever-present and always at hand for us to pour out the situations that pain us the most.

"Uh-oh," we remember.

"I know," God says. "I know. I was there. I'm here still."

When my mom learned in her childhood that God was always present, always watching, she pictured him as a cosmic hall monitor just waiting for her to mess up. Later, she realized God's omnipresence wasn't a threat but a promise. "I will never leave you or forsake you" didn't mean you had better behave; it meant you always had someone who shared your experience, your memories. Someone who understood.

Community as the Antidote to Forgetting

God wants us to remember so we'll remember we're not alone. But forgetting seems to be one thing we humans do best.

Forgetting takes no effort at all. You can forget without even trying. It's remembering that makes us work for it. In junior high, I kept leaving behind my designer denim jacket in classrooms or in the gym after a pep rally or at the local pizza joint. My mom made me go back and find it again and again, until one day it wasn't there. She bought me a new one, a replacement worth less money and less teenage status, and she lowered its cool factor even further by writing my name and phone number in large-lettered permanent marker across the inner lining. I never lost the replacement, even though I frequently wished I could as I carried it carefully folded over my arm so no one would spot my name and phone number inside. I needed that permanent marker to force me to remember, because forgetting was so easy.

Our memories grow with us. The more life we've lived, the more years to remember. But as we age, even into young adulthood, life gets more complex and complicated, with more balls to juggle and more experiences to store, and so our memory needs help. We make lists and install apps that ping us with notifications to remember things. Some childhood memories begin to grow fuzzy over the years. We can no longer recall the name of the dog we'd pet each day at the bus stop or the kid we sat by in the lunchroom, even if it was for one hundred days straight. By the time we have kids of our own, the chaos of living life—of adulting itself—starts to push out some of the details connected to memories that might have mattered most: the first kiss, first Communion, first time moving away from home.

Memory is like a muscle we build. It grows in childhood, and we expect it will continue to gain strength as we learn new facts and skills along the way. But like other muscles, there is some tipping point at which we begin to lose strength, lose memory, even feel like we're losing ourselves. We know from those who suffer with short-term memory loss or devastating dementia just how chaotic life without memory can be. To lose memory is not just to lose stories, but to lose connections as well. Relationships.

Identity. Take the pins out of the map that mark where you've been and you find yourself lost, even if you're standing in the exact same spot. The less we remember, the more we need our circle tightening around us to keep our pins in place. Just as a parent might walk through the house with a baby and name things to spark new memories, that baby might grow up to sit with an aging parent, rehearsing memories to strengthen them. *Light. Fan. Star. Something happened here.*

When stories are important enough, they last through generations as an unexpected gift. When they are told, something more than an anecdote is preserved. If they disappear, something unnamed is lost. Families often pass unique pieces of their stories from generation to generation, either with smiles of shared recognition or maybe with the pursed lips of judgment or the knitted brows of regret. We aren't born knowing our stories. We have to be told them.

I sat holding a glass at a wedding reception recently and listened as person after person stood up and toasted the bride and groom. All of the toasts started by looking back, even as we wished the couple on to the future they had just spoken of in their vows just an hour before. College friends told stories of shared shenanigans. Childhood friends evoked embarrassing and endearing memories. Each toast seemed to go further and further back into their history. First recent friendships, then friends and family going back decades, then their parents. But then the grandfather of the bride stood up. "I've only known Tyler a year or so, but I first met Callie twenty-five years ago," he said. "I held her in my arms and said to her, 'We've waited a long time for you, girl." His son, the father of the bride, let the tears he had been choking back all day spill over. This was a moment where generations were knit together by shared stories. A day the bride could never have recalled on her own was evoked and connected to a day she would never forget. We all raised our glasses to that.

Remembering is a gift we give to each other. Glancing back means pointing to the pins in each other's maps, marking memory and story and connection. The old do this when they share their stories with the young, and then later, when memory is fading, the young return the favor for the old.

Where chaos lurks and threatens, our connectedness pulls us back from the brink with the bonds that remind us of who we are. God is exceptional at this role, calling us again and again to remember our story, whispering hints of the foundation of our identity, going so far back that no living person can tell it.

Called to Remember

When God rescued his people from slavery in Egypt, he knew this would become their defining story—not just the story of a lifetime but of all of their lifetimes to come. Their slavery had lasted four hundred long years, so the memory of being rescued needed to stretch out in front of them the way the story of being enslaved reached back—deep and defining. Four hundred years is long enough to make you forget you've ever been anything but slaves. To forget the feeling of the freedom to make your own decisions, your own money, a life you can call your own. After four hundred years, the whip scars are etched so deep that you might just forget the story of how you came to be strangers in a strange land.

It was, in fact, forgetting that had made them slaves in the first place. Their ancestor Joseph, attacked by jealous brothers who didn't like it that their dad gave him a special coat and special attention, ended up in Egypt by accident when they faked his death and sold him to slave traders. Joseph didn't stay a slave for long, rising through the ranks of Egyptian government to save all of Egypt from a famine. The grateful pharaoh made him his second-in-command. When Joseph's eleven brothers, brought to their knees in repentance by starvation and regret, all moved to Egypt with their families too, the family multiplied and multiplied over the generations until a new pharaoh looked out at the growing crowds of Israelites and saw a burgeoning multitude of potential servitude. He had pyramids dancing in his dreams and knew he'd need a workforce of slave labor to get it done.

This pharaoh didn't know and didn't care that they all descended from Joseph's little troubled family. He didn't care that Joseph had saved the nation once upon a time. Joseph who? It was the loss of their story, the lack of memory, that put them in this awful predicament. Off came the shiny coat and on went four hundred years of sackcloth, brick dust, and whip scars.

God heard the cries of his people who had been enslaved for all those generations and made a spectacle out of their rescue. It was meant to be unforgettable. "Let my people go!" Moses stuttered, and when Pharaoh laughed at the very thought, God let Pharaoh know that he meant business, raining chaos in plague after plague. The Israelites avoided the last and most devastating plague, the death of the firstborn child in every family, by painting the blood of a lamb over their doors so death would pass over. Pharaoh told them to get out and good riddance, but when he changed his mind and chased them up against the Red Sea, God parted it like a hot knife through butter and sent his people through, drowning Pharaoh, his men, and the horses right behind them. When God got them all out alive, he wanted them to return thanks in the form of memory.

Remember, he would tell them. *Remember the chaos. Remember that you were once slaves in Egypt. Then remember how the Lord your God rescued you. Remember that God is bigger than the pharaoh, bigger than the sea, bigger than any chaos that blocks your way to the future or chases you from the past.*

Having witnessed spectacular and powerful acts on their behalf, you'd think holding on to the memory of such a dramatic story would be easy, but it wasn't. Chaos in the present can make the chaos of the past blur with nostalgia until it begins to seem appealing. Enticing, even. First God's people forgot just how bad it all was. When the chaos of traveling through the wilderness was too much to bear, they began to recall just how good things were back in Egypt. *In Egypt there was always meat to eat. Always water to drink. In Egypt no one made us march through a hot, sandy desert day after day. Remember how great we had it?* The chaos of the desert began to take the edge off the memory of how bad the chaos of slavery had truly been.

Response

A friend of mine grew up in Cold War Russia. In elementary school, they practiced bombing drills by climbing under their desks. They called Americans dirty and cruel. On the other side of the world, American kids were huddled under their desks, saying the same about them. My friend remembers the days when Communism fell. There was rejoicing for a while, but it didn't take long for forgetfulness to slip in. "Remember back in the days when everything was provided for us?" people would say to each other. "Back then, the government gave us everything we needed—food and clothing and shelter too. Now we're left to fend for ourselves!" My friend remembered those days too, but he also remembered the fear, the scarcity, and the long lines just to get bread or clothing for their family.

Weren't the good old days of Communism great?
Remember what we had back in Egypt? Those were the days.

First God's people forgot how bad it was. Then they forgot how good God was. Once they got beyond the bonds of Egypt, Moses headed up a mountain to ask God just what he was supposed to do with all these people. Meanwhile, in the shadow of that same mountain, God's people were throwing gold and jewels into a fire to make a tiny, shiny golden calf and declare, "These are your gods, Israel, who brought you up out of Egypt" (Exodus 32:4).

Losing our memories of how bad things were always means losing sight of how good God has been. We may not want to remember the hard times, but God's goodness that pulled us through them is too important a memory to forget. And the two are always connected.

The Israelites had called out in desperation under the

yoke of slavery and God heard and rescued them. But when they lost the memory of how desperately they had sought God's help, they danced around a fire and lifted out an idol to give it credit for the work God had done. If only they had remembered their desperation as slaves! If only they had returned to that memory and acknowledged what God did for them. If they had just tapped into the power of memory to order chaos, they might have turned to him instead of an idol. They might have slipped to safety under God's umbrella of grace, grateful for his work in their lives—grateful for God himself.

Remember, God continued to whisper. *Remember you were slaves. Remember I rescued you.* He whispered and then shouted it. Commanded and then begged. He wrote it in permanent ink inside their jackets. *Don't misplace this*, God said. *Look behind you to be sure you haven't left it. If you don't remember where you came from, what's to prevent you from wandering back there again? You don't have to be slaves to seek me; you just have to remember that you once were.*

Since God knew the way to his people's hearts was through their taste buds, he even created a meal to jog their memories every year. He called it the Passover to connect them with the moment of the last and worst plague in Egypt when death passed over their doors because of the blood of a sacrificed lamb. At this meal they would eat lamb, taste bitter herbs and salty water, and remember bitterness and tears. At this meal they would rehearse the whole story, their slavery in Egypt, their desperate cries, God's answer, and their journey to freedom. *Remember*, they would say to each other over full plates and full bellies. *Remember when you didn't have any of this but only God and each other. Love him today like you did that day. Don't lose your devotion when you lose your desperation. Taste your memories from this plate. Live them over and over as if they're happening fresh again. Every time you eat this meal. Every year. Remember.*

This meal of memories was supposed to keep their hearts and lives ordered to remember and give thanks and worship. It was precisely the chaos that they had been through that would drive them into God's arms again and again, the chaos of the past preparing them for any chaos in the future by reminding them that only God the Creator holds the universe in his hands and only God the Rescuer can hold them close during whatever disaster or disruption may come in it. The meal included a story, the memory—the truth—of how God set them free. And just because they were freed once didn't mean the story stopped there for them, or for us.

The Truth Will Set You Free

Forgetting can be accidental. The name that slips our mind. The denim jacket left behind in the classroom. But sometimes we forget because we let go of a past we don't want to be reminded of, one that isn't the identity we want to call forward and claim for our present, much less take with us into the future. But when we forget, we unintentionally welcome in the chaos that comes when we disconnect from a past that pairs struggle with resilience, crisis with rescue.

We see this clearly in the gospel of John. Jesus was talking to some Jews—some members of the larger family that traced their lineage back to slavery and plagues and parted seas. These people of the Passover story were listening eagerly to what Jesus was saying, so he offered them a next step: "If you hold to my teaching, you are really my disciples. Then you will know the truth, and the truth will set you free" (John 8:31–32).

It was as if a loud bang interrupted the conversation and created an awkward, echoing pause. Uh-oh. Just the mention of freedom somehow deeply offended them. For Jesus to say that they needed freedom implied they weren't already free. So they retorted, "We are Abraham's descendants and have never been slaves of anyone. How can you say that we shall be set free?" (John 8:33).

We have never been slaves of anyone. Seriously? Four hundred years of bricks and whips and scars have evaporated into the air of self-confident self-reliance. No slavery. No rescue. No telling the story of the incredible acts of God. No need to depend on anyone but yourself now.

Why couldn't they follow Jesus? Because they couldn't remember. Or rather, they wouldn't. Even though they ate the Passover meal and swallowed the memories of their people every single year, they couldn't identify with the emaciated and oppressed bodies of slaves subservient to Egyptian masters. But when they blocked out the memory of chaos, they missed the memory of the compassionate, rescuing God who was now standing in person right before their faces.

Here was Jesus, ready to rescue—offering his blood so

that the threat of death born back in the garden would pass over once again. Here was Jesus, standing at the Red Sea, offering to part the waters through baptism. Would they bite? *No thanks*, they said. *We don't recall ever being slaves. We're just fine as we are, thanks. We've edited the memory of our story so that we don't have to depend on anyone but ourselves, Jesus. You keep your rescue for somebody who really needs it.*

The Bible is full of stories people would rather not tell—prostitutes in the family tree, denials and betrayals at just the wrong crucial moments, darkness and death and abandonment on a cross. If we cut out these stories, we don't get to remember the next chapters. Our memory of a swirling, chaotic past redeemed by God is the only thing that makes us desperate enough to follow him to a clearer future.

We'll never remember it all alone, so God calls us to remind each other often. We remember our sins corporately in words of confession. We say the Lord's Prayer as a family—*our* Father, not just *my* Father. We eat bread and drink wine and find ourselves standing together in remembrance, our voices joining in unison with every saint, living and dead, all present together at the Lord's table. Our memory is vast, our voice united. When we speak together, chaos cannot touch it.

In Remembrance of Me

A pastor friend of mine and her husband were driving through California on vacation and found themselves visiting a small Episcopal church one Sunday morning.

Being a pastor who visits other churches is like being a backseat driver in every single worship service you attend. When things go well, your brain is busy taking notes of parts to imitate and repeat back in your own church. When things go wrong, you can't help but mentally correct them. It takes a great deal of mental energy just to turn off your "leader brain" and become a participant in the pew.

As my friend settled into her pew and willed herself just to listen and sing and absorb this particular day of worship, the service began to fall apart. First, the priest lost his place in the sermon. It took him a while to find his footing again, and he repeated quite a bit before he managed to move on. This happened more than once.

Then as the comfortingly familiar words of the Communion liturgy were unfolding in rhythmic progression, the priest lost his place again. And again. He stopped and fumbled and then started back in at the wrong spot. It was such a mess that the congregation actually began speaking the parts meant for the leader loudly just to prompt him and keep the service going.

My friend found the chaos unnerving.

As the service ended and she and her husband collected themselves to leave, a woman from the congregation approached them warmly with words of welcome. Then she lowered her voice and added with a kind smile, "Our service isn't usually this disjointed, but our priest has early-onset Alzheimer's disease. When he forgets his part, we read for him until he remembers and joins in again."

My pastor friend was stunned.

What she had witnessed wasn't a disaster; it was a

community. What she assumed was a failure at doing church was actually the church at its best. Here was a church that didn't demand perfection. They didn't discard their pastor as soon as things got rough. They were loving him through deep weakness and struggle, raising their voices as his own declined. The flock was leading the shepherd, walking alongside him and helping him stay on course. Sticking beside him even as his own mind betrayed him.

The words of liturgy we say in church can seem strange at times. Repetitive. Monotonous. Someone who had very little experience going to church once whispered to me on the way out of the service, "What are all these words we say at the same time?" When you haven't recited anything but the Pledge of Allegiance in unison before, matching the cadence of other voices to echo words that are not your own can be intimidating. But liturgy, particularly the words said standing before the altar that is set with the holy gifts of Communion, works on us best over time. Repetition can be both monotonous and meaningful. A spouse's daily kiss on the cheek on the way out the door condenses a lifetime of love into a repetitive habit. Its meaning is deep even if we aren't deeply remembering its meaning every time.

After dozens of times reciting those holy words in a shower of other voices at the Communion table, liturgy wears a groove in us, creates a memory where none existed before. We are disciples sitting with Jesus around a table, eating the ancient Passover meal, when suddenly he changes the script, and we are shocked at his declaration: "This is my body. This is my blood." We behold the Lamb of God come to take away the sins of the world, even mine.

We are slaves, transported back to the first Passover, painting the blood of a pet lamb now sacrificed over our doors and holding our breath to see if death will pass over. We walk out the next morning breathing free air and pass through the sea unscathed, rescued, redeemed. These are memories that are real in us, not because we were present, but because the Holy Spirit brings the past rushing forward and makes it our story. The miracles of tables past kiss us on the cheek like a spouse on the way out the door, and we are made whole.

Under the Umbrella of God's Grace

Ask most people to remember the hardest thing they've been through in life, and there's usually a deep story of gratitude of some kind connected to it—gratitude that they survived, that life is better now. Christians hold tightly to gratitude that God brought them through their chaos—even if wasn't a sea or a plague or an army with chariots—because it's the deepest difficulties of our lives that uncover God's power, his mercy, his rescue. Sometimes the desperation we felt during those experiences was the very thing that drove us into the arms of Jesus. Chaos forced us to seek a way out, and God was there to rescue us.

If chaos sends us running into the arms of God, should we seek it every day? If you ask me, I'd rather not. But this is the beautiful thing about memory. It allows us to connect with those moments long after they've happened. It reminds us that we don't have to lead a desperate life to benefit from a desperate heart. Just knowing how much we need God—remembering the days, weeks, and months we woke to chaotic thoughts, relationships, or situations—will take our hearts to that place where we acknowledge our need for him. We remember how good God was when we were in the pit of despair and feel grateful. Our gratitude for his work in the past connects us to God without having to be in the pit today. Remembering our hardest moments means we can acknowledge that we need God on our best day just as much as we did on our worst. The residue of the chaos is enough to drive us under God's umbrella of grace even when the skies are clear.

Sometimes when memory fails, when we lose our place and have to start again, when the stars are falling in our lives, the other voices rise as our voice falters and speak the truth for us even when we can't. Chaos comes into the lives of all of us from time to time. But even after we recover our balance, we shouldn't forget it. It's the connections we've made that hold our place on the page, that keep us following along, until we find our place again.

Chapter 8

CHOSEN CHAOS

The Mel Fisher Maritime Museum in Key West, Florida, is devoted to a normal guy with an extraordinary dream.

Mel Fisher grew up on an Indiana chicken farm. As a farm kid, he read *Treasure Island* and was hooked. He wanted to live his life seeking adventure and finding lost treasure. The first chance he got, he left his landlocked hometown and moved to California, where he learned to scuba dive and opened the very first dive shop in the state. He bought some basic equipment and borrowed a boat to head out to a few areas where there had been supposed shipwrecks, but he found nothing. Again and again his dives turned up empty, but instead of giving up, he doubled down on his dream, moving his wife and five children to Florida so he could pursue treasure hunting full-time.

The Fisher family was determined to find one historic shipwreck, the mysteriously vanished Spanish galleon ship named the *Nuestra Señora de Atocha*. The *Atocha* sank in 1622 in the waters just off the coast of the Florida Keys, taking more than $400 million in treasure with her into the depths.

Mel and his wife and five children, now young adults, spent every penny on their dream. They collected thousands from investors to buy or rent the specialized equipment they needed to search. They even lived on a leaky houseboat, selling every possession that could get them funds to put them one step closer to finding the treasure.

Over the years, most of those who had joined Mel in his search dropped out, discouraged or depleted of funds. But as others gave up hope, Fisher's faith seemed to grow every day he searched. He was relentless, determined. He started each day by announcing to his small crew, "Today's the day!" It became his credo. He truly believed that each day he launched could be the day they would find treasure.

Eventually he became a laughingstock, even among other treasure hunters. Who continues to search, day after day, without any evidence that you're any closer to what you're searching for? Who gives up every other comfort, every other priority, in pursuit of a singular thing that no one else seems to believe is attainable? His response to the barrage of ridicule was to wake every morning with the same relentless optimism and the same motto: "Today's the day!"

Finally, after six years of searching and thousands of dives, tragedy struck. On July 20, 1975, Mel's oldest son, Dirk; Dirk's wife, Angel; and a fellow diver were out on a dive, hunting for the wreck, when their boat capsized. All three of them drowned. In his quest for treasure, Mel lost his firstborn son.

"Surely," people said, "this man will quit this insanity now. Surely he will come to his senses." Do you know what Mel said? "Today's the day." And he set out to search again.

Mel Fisher spent another ten years searching. He poured a total of sixteen years and hundreds of thousands of dollars into his quest to unearth the *Atocha* and the priceless treasure buried with her. For more than five thousand days, Mel told himself, his crew, and the world that "today's the day" he would finally achieve his dream. And finally he was right.

Ten years to the day after he lost his son and daughter-in-law at sea, on July 20, 1985, Mel Fisher and his team discovered the wreck of the *Atocha*. At an estimated $450 million in value, it was one of the most valuable shipwrecks recovered in history. It included 40 tons of gold and silver and some of the finest gems in the world. The Colombian emeralds found on the *Atocha* are so remarkable that they are now the world's standard by which all emeralds are judged.

The United States government tried to lay claim to the treasure Mel had found, and they fought all the way to the Supreme Court. After an eight-year court battle, the final ruling was "finders keepers." So Mel Fisher got the payload he had given his life to search for—or, more accurately, what was left after his lawyers and investors were paid.

Instead of hanging up his diving suit, Mel Fisher used his reward to invest in more equipment and hire more crew, and then he launched out again. His discovery, though vast, was roughly only half of the treasure that went down with the *Atocha*, and he was convinced today was the day he might find the other half, the wealthiest part of the ship. The stern castle, as it is known, is still lying undiscovered somewhere on the ocean floor to this day.

Today, a large rock in front of the museum devoted to Mel Fisher bears the engraving, "Today's the Day."

Treasure Comes at a Cost

The story of Mel and his family and their quest stirred a memory deep inside me of another treasure-hunting story. Jesus told it like this: "The kingdom of heaven is like treasure hidden in a field. When a man found it, he hid it again, and then in his joy went and sold all he had and bought that field" (Matthew 13:44).

That's it. That's the story.

Instead of telling us the story of how this man searched, sacrificed, and failed, Jesus simply starts his story at the moment the man finds the treasure. We don't even really know if he's been looking for it or if he just stumbles on it. Maybe he's just passing through the field and gets lucky. Maybe he's a day laborer who uncovers the treasure in a field where he's been hired to work. In any case, he doesn't run out and announce his discovery to the world. He shrewdly hides the treasure, makes a plan to possess it as soon as possible, and sets off to put his plan into action.

First, he liquidates his assets. He sells everything he has—his home, his investments, any animals or means of transportation he had, the clothes in his closet and the shirt off his back. He sells it. All of it.

There is no halfway with this kind of treasure. You either give it all or nothing. Things that are worth a lot cost a lot. Things that are going to be worth everything cost everything, and this treasure cost the man everything he owned.

One cost the story doesn't mention is the cost of his reputation. What did people think when he began selling all his possessions? What did his neighbors whisper about him? How many well-meaning family members tried to intervene, thinking he had lost his mind? Did he have a wife? Did she care when he sold the couch, the table, their home out from under her? Choosing to pursue his dream of treasure must have thrown this man's life into utter chaos: The chaos of disruption from selling off his creature comforts. The chaos of alienation from those who just didn't understand.

By choosing the treasure, this man is choosing chaos. But the treasure itself is worth the chaos it will take to get to it.

As he looks around at everything he's ever valued, he counts it all as rubbish, worthless, except for the one goal of acquiring the thing of great worth in front of him. And he holds a rubbish sale. And he counts out the profit in his hand, one penny at a time, holding his breath to be sure it's enough.

And he buys the land.

And he starts digging.

The story ends before the moment we're really waiting for. We don't get to hear about the joy of buying the field or digging up the treasure or bringing it home. We don't get to hear about family and friends finding out the man wasn't completely bonkers when he sold all he had. The only joy we get to hear described is the joy of pursuit. Even in the chaos of turning his life upside down, we're told, "In his joy [he] went and sold all he had."

Next, Jesus tells the same story all over again, only this time with different characters: "Again, the kingdom of heaven is like a merchant looking for fine pearls. When he found one of great value, he went away and sold everything he had and bought it" (Matthew 13:45–46).

In this new version, the merchant does not blindly stumble on anything. He is out looking for fine pearls when he finds this one. You might say he's a professional treasure hunter. He has a practiced method, a discerning eye. But for all the pearls he's ever seen, for all the ones he has acquired for his collection and sold to other collectors, he has never seen anything like this one. This is the pearl of a lifetime.

While other gems are dug up or scratched from the walls of a mine after forming under pressure, a pearl is the only one produced by a living organism. An oyster forms a pearl in response to an intrusion. Something slips inside its armored shell and lands in its mantle, its soft inner tissue. It can be the tiniest of intrusions, or maybe even an injury or illness. For us it would be like a splinter in our skin or even a speck of dust in our eye. For the oyster it might be a broken piece of its own shell, a grain of sand, or some tiny bacteria that happened to rub it the wrong way. Something makes its life miserable, so the oyster makes it beautiful.

The oyster can't let something scratch up its soft insides, so it surrounds them with something called a pearl sac, a membrane that encloses the irritant and begins bathing it in a substance called nacre, the same substance that coats the shell's insides in shiny mother-of-pearl. It applies layer after smooth, beautiful layer for years until what's inside no longer looks or feels like an irritant, but becomes a beautiful gem, a pearl.

Think about it for a moment. Isn't it amazing that something so beautiful can start out as an irritant or injury? If you were an oyster, the great prize of your life might be something that started out as your greatest pain. In the economy of God, sometimes your wounds become your greatest gifts. That'll preach.

And this particular oyster, the one Jesus is telling the story about, has produced the greatest response to an irritant or imperfection that anyone has ever seen. Our merchant, even though he's seen a million pearls before, is still blown away by what he finds. So he does something that by now seems quite familiar to us: he goes and joyfully sells everything else he has—he liquidates all his assets—for the joy of possessing this one thing. He chooses the chaos of pursuit over the stability of sameness.

Again, there is no going halfway for this kind of treasure. If you want it, you have to give it your all. Throw everything you once valued into the pot. This is a once-in-a-lifetime chance.

Things that are worth a lot cost a lot. Things that are worth everything cost everything.

The Chaotic Path of Pursuing Jesus

Paul famously said of the life he built before he met Jesus that he counted everything "rubbish" for the sake of following Christ (Philippians 3:8 ESV). The word translated "rubbish" is really the word *dung*. Paul is saying that, compared to the treasure of Christ, everything the world ever offered him is a load of crap. (Don't frown at me—it's in the Bible!)

For those who have discovered the treasure of Jesus, this means if we have to choose between anything else and Christ, we will choose Christ. And there's a whole lot of "anything else" out there! Not only possessions, but reputation, career, status, control.

Choosing Christ means choosing the right thing, but the right thing is often the harder thing. "Holy disruption," we sometimes call it. Following Jesus means a narrower path with more twists and turns, but choosing a path is more about choosing a destination than an easy road.

I've met so many people who have sold it all to pursue the treasure. They don't usually seem out of the ordinary until you hear their stories. One told me he refused to inflate the quarterly numbers at work, so they refused him a promotion. Instead he found treasure in Christ. Another sat in the car and refused to go in when her college friends surprised her with a trip to a strip club. She was rewarded with ridicule. And treasure in Christ.

A family in our neighborhood with two teen boys and a daughter in elementary school kept feeling the tug toward foster parenting. Their desire was definitely not born out of excess—their home was already crowded and their finances tight. Excess time wasn't something they had on their hands either. They were barely able to find the time for the extensive trainings and certifications required to become a foster family. But then a baby boy was brought to their front door, one who had been born into circumstances filled with chaos through no choice of his own. They opened their door wide and welcomed the chaos in.

Representative John Lewis of Georgia was someone who chose chaos for the common good. Reflecting on how Rosa Parks's example had inspired him, he said, "She inspired us to find a way, to get in the way, to get in what I call good trouble, necessary trouble . . . And for people if you see something that is not right, not fair, not just, do something. We cannot afford to be quiet."[15] Lewis ended up joining Dr. Martin Luther King Jr. in leading the Civil Rights Movement. "Good trouble" in the face of injustice is still a calling, but one that means choosing chaos in the face of forces that call for quiet.

Following Jesus doesn't guarantee less chaos. Often it brings more. Jesus was pretty clear about that. "Take up your cross and follow me" is not a verse often sold framed in calligraphy in Christian stores. "In this world you will have trouble" is not a promise many people claim as their life verse. The other half of Jesus' saying—"But take heart! I have overcome the world"—is comforting, but still doesn't explain when things will get better. Choosing Jesus means choosing chaos because it means we choose to swim his way against the chaotic current around us instead of floating along with it. It takes a little practice sometimes to realize that experiencing resistance doesn't mean you're doing it wrong. Jesus himself is proof that life without resistance was not the goal in the first place. Mel Fisher is not the only one to face the death of a firstborn son in pursuit of treasure.

Today's the Day

I was so inspired by Mel Fisher's story that I couldn't get it out of my head. One Kentucky winter morning, I shared it with a chapel full of seminary students, preaching it alongside Jesus' two short stories—the treasure and the pearl. I called the sermon "Today's the Day" and closed by asking people if anything from the rubbish pile had crept into their treasure box. If so, I told them, "today's the day" to have a rubbish sale and begin pursuing the treasure of God wholeheartedly again.

That afternoon, I met with a young female student. She greeted me politely but seemed a little shaky, her face white and her voice almost a whisper. She was clutching a journal as she sat down in one of the chairs facing each other near the window.

"I almost canceled on you," she started slowly, "but then I heard your sermon this morning." Then she took a deep breath, and it all tumbled out. "See, I need to confess something. Last semester I cheated on a test. It was stupid, really. I was swamped with classes and work and just didn't take time to prepare. We were supposed to take the test at home, and we were told not to look at our books or notes. We had to sign a statement at the end of our work saying we had not cracked a book while the test was in progress. But when I opened the test, there were all of these questions I had no idea how to answer. I knew right where the information was in my notes, so, almost without thinking, I looked it up. I looked at my notes to find answers to more than half of the questions. Then at the end, I signed the statement and turned it in, relieved to be done and thinking it was over." She shook her head sadly. "But ever since, it's like it's been haunting me. I deceived my professor. I got a grade I didn't deserve. Now I'm miserable. Whenever people tell me it's so great that I'm going into ministry, I think, *If you only knew who I really am and what I've done, you wouldn't think I'm all that great.* So I needed to tell someone. And now I have. And now I guess you're going to say I have to go and tell my professor too. And I'll probably get kicked out of school and have to leave all of this behind."

She sat in tearful silence for a moment as I passed her the tissue box.

"First of all," I said, "I'm just so proud of you for coming today. It took a lot of courage to come in and admit what you did. You said you almost canceled today," I reminded her. "What changed your mind?"

She paused and opened the journal she had been white-knuckling on her lap. "This is what I wrote in my journal before I'd heard your sermon at chapel this morning."

She handed me the notebook, where in flowing cursive she had written, "I can't live like this anymore. I'm finally going to do what's right, no matter how hard it is, no matter what happens because of it. I have to start living the way I know God is calling me to live, and this will be the start. I'll go confess today and see where this leads, but no matter what, I know I can't turn back." Under this, in big, bold script, underlined three times, were the words: "TODAY'S THE DAY." She had written them before she ever heard these exact words in my sermon.

"See," she said, "I almost canceled and just kept hiding, but then I heard those words in your sermon this morning. It's like God was talking right to me! That story about giving up everything to go after the one right thing—that's me."

As hard as it was, she knew she was selling the rubbish for the one true thing of value; she was trading the dung for treasure. The chaos in the short term—confessing to her professor, facing the consequences—would be worth it if she could just hold on for the ride. She did, and she ended up taking the test over and getting a lower grade in the class, but what she gained was sweeter than what she gave up.

The Hunted Treasure

A parable is a sneaky thing. Sometimes you can be listening to one of Jesus' nice, predictable stories, and all of a sudden it will flip on you. Things change suddenly, and the character you assumed you were in the story is not who you are at all.

Suddenly you're a priest passing by an injured man on the side of the road.

Or an older brother, pouting outside on the porch while the party rages on inside.

These tiny little stories of the hidden treasure and the fine pearl are no exception. They're tricky things, these little stories that seem so obvious at first glance.

"The kingdom of heaven is like a treasure hidden in a field," Jesus says.

That's elementary, Jesus. Grade school stuff. We all know

the kingdom is a treasure. We find it. We sell all we have.
We get it. Life is good.

"Okay," says Jesus. "Again. Let's try this one again, only this time, 'The kingdom of heaven is like a merchant.'"

Wait a minute, Jesus. You just said the kingdom was a treasure, something we seek after. But a merchant? A merchant is someone who does the seeking. If God's kingdom is the merchant in this story, if God is the one doing the seeking and finding, then who am I?

"Oh," Jesus says. "Oh, didn't you know? You're the pearl."

Once there was a gardener who already owned a field. It was a garden actually, and it was a beautiful one. He had all the treasure he could want there. The world was his oyster.

And into that oyster of a world came an irritant, an intrusion. It was a splinter under the skin, a speck of dust in the eye, an injury to creation that changed the shape of the world forever. It was a broken piece where there had been no brokenness before.

It ate the fruit. Killed the brother. Built the tower. Brought a cascade of sin flooding in to make the inhabitable uninhabitable, the light darkness, the order chaos. It caused injury and irritation over and over and over again—not just to others, but to itself too.

And instead of casting it out, instead of spitting it into the abyss, instead of finding creation horribly scratched beyond repair, the gardener found a new way to bring order to the chaos. He embraced it, surrounded it with himself, and made it beautiful.

In one layer after another around our gritty, broken selves, Jesus enfolded us with grace, so that the roughest parts would turn out the most beautiful. In God's economy, our wounds would become our greatest gifts.

We are the pearl. We may think we're a merchant out hunting, selling all we've acquired and losing our reputation to gain the one important thing. But we cannot seek harder than we have already been sought. We cannot give up more for God than he has already given for us.

Jesus is the treasure hunter. We are the pearl.

God sought treasure with the total abandon of all he possessed. And we were that treasure. All of his stories confirm it—the shepherd hunting for a lost sheep, the woman frantically searching for a lost coin, the man who threw a party when his lost son returned. We once were lost, but now are found.

A Chaotic Pursuit

If we think we've encountered chaos in our quest to follow Jesus, imagine the chaos he went through to get to us. The story of Jesus' quest for reconciliation with us, his lost treasure, makes the plot of Mel Fisher's saga look as simple as a Saturday morning cartoon.

When Jesus stepped out of heaven to take on human flesh, it was certainly a departure from the comforts of a heavenly throne. Jesus not only took on a body prone to hunger, tiredness, and physical discomfort, but he also became vulnerable to sickness, injury, and even death. To fully adopt humanity, he had to adopt not only the good but the bad as well.

On December 26, 2004, a tsunami struck Indonesia, Sri Lanka, and surrounding countries. Initial news reports guessed the death toll might have been around 10,000. They were more than a little off: at least 225,000 people died in the tragedy.[16]

The numbers and scope are hard to even imagine. Entire coastlines were wiped off the map; towns were destroyed; families searched desperately for news of loved ones. The chaos rising up from dark and troubled waters seemed, well, biblical in scope. Sometimes it was the individual stories, names, pictures, narratives of loss that brought home the immense impact. One particular picture stuck in my head and has never left.

That Christmas morning, Karen Svaerd and her family were enjoying their vacation in Thailand, a contrast from the winter they had left behind at home in Sweden. That morning as they were all out swimming in the water, Karen turned toward the ocean and saw the tsunami wave approaching. She looked from it to her family members in the surf, who were facing the beach and had no idea what was behind them. Her whole world was frozen there for a moment in the foamy waves—her husband, Lars; her sons Anton (fourteen), Filip (eleven), and Viktor (ten); and her brother, Per, unaware that hell itself was bearing down just behind them.

Someone snapped a photo that captured this moment, and here's what I'll never forget. In the freeze-frame, Karen is turned with her back to the camera, running toward her family, running toward disaster and death. In every other picture of the tragedy that day, every person who became aware of what was about to happen was running *away* from the danger; Karen was running *toward* it. Someone on the beach said she was yelling, "Oh, my God, not my children!"

For days, all the world knew about the family was their breathtaking picture. It went viral as people struggled to comprehend the weight of the loss the world had suffered in individual stories. Several days later, one of the family members was reading a report about the tragedy and saw their own picture in the international news with the caption, "No One Knows If They Survived." They contacted reporters to deliver the incredible news: the whole family lived.

"I can remember the white foam, how the surf took them up and they disappeared," Karen said later in an interview. "I could hear people shouting at me 'Get off the beach' as I ran past them—but I ignored them," she said. "I had to try and save my children, nothing was going to stop me."[17]

They were all lifted in the wave but landed safely and separated. They spent what felt like forever calling and searching for each other, and then they finally discovered they had all made it out alive.

That image of Karen surrounded by people fleeing the other way, running desperately toward danger, toward the people she loved most, made my breath catch in my throat and my eyes blur. It reminded me of Jesus.

If you want to see a picture of someone choosing chaos over calm for the sake of a treasure, that picture is Jesus. Death had us in its jaws, and Jesus ran straight for us. *Not my children!* you can almost hear him saying. But to run toward death meant giving his own life for ours.

The letter to the Hebrews says it this way: "For the joy

set before him he endured the cross" (Hebrews 12:2). That anticipatory joy in the face of chaos, disruption, and pain sounds a lot like the joy of the treasure hunter and the joy of the merchant, knowing that on the other side of chaos is a treasure worth abandoning it all for.

The great hymn writer Charles Wesley described Jesus' self-abandoning run toward chaos and death this way:

> He left his Father's throne above,
> (So free, so infinite his grace!)
> Empty'd himself of all but love,
> And bled for Adam's helpless race:
> 'Tis mercy all, immense and free!
> For O my God! It found out me![18]

God is powerful enough to run straight toward death to rescue his children and emerge victorious in the end, his treasure safely restored.

You. You are the treasure. You are the pearl. You were worth it to him.

Chapter 9

UNDIVIDED

Imagine you're in church.

That may not be a big stretch of the imagination. Perhaps you've been there often, maybe even recently.

But the church you're imagining now is the church of the 60s. Not the 1960s, just the 60s. AD 60. Now you know why you needed to bring your imagination.

In AD 60, there was no such thing as a church building. So we've gathered in someone's home, the entirety of it probably smaller than most modern living rooms and definitely containing less. Children dart between people's legs, and the host gets up to shoo a family chicken out the door from time to time. Chaos bubbles and calms. We sit on the floor to worship and to eat, since there's always a meal when we're together, and it always culminates in the Lord's Supper. More than a little morsel of bread and sip of wine, it leaves us full, satisfied, and prepared to serve and feed others.

We all bring what we have for the meal. Some of us have a lot to offer, some very little. When we leave at the end, things have been evened out a bit—some go with their pockets lighter and some with their purses filled.

We're all recent converts to the faith, all of us first-generation believers. Our families didn't follow the Way, but we do. We've been captivated by the stories of this Jesus who healed and taught, who himself suffered and died and was raised from the dead. It's all we want to talk about when we're together, but we're careful how loudly we say it. The Roman emperor has ears everywhere. The messages Jesus taught were so threatening to the empire that they executed him, and that has us looking over our shoulders to see who might be listening. If they find our gatherings threatening, they might kill us too.

But even with the fear of Roman oppression hanging over us like a cloud, there is a buzz of excitement about today's gathering. Because today, a letter has arrived, and we're dying to find out what's in it. This is the kind of letter that's not written to one person, but to everyone in our region who follows the Way. It's been circulating among the little house churches like ours, being passed secretly under baskets and cloaks in the market, and now it's our turn—and we can't wait to read it.

Most of us can't read, but there are one or two who have a little education because of a higher status or who have picked up a few things from the shopkeepers they work for. One of them stands now and reads in a loud, clear voice:

> Therefore, remember that formerly you who are Gentiles by birth and called "uncircumcised" by those who call themselves "the circumcision" (which is done in the body by human hands)—remember that at that time you were separate from Christ, excluded from citizenship in Israel and foreigners to the covenants of the promise, without hope and without God in the world.
>
> *Ephesians 2:11–12*

Boy, do we remember! It's not long ago we were living life lost and without hope. Those words hit close to home because when we first heard about the hope found in Jesus, we also heard that we would have to become Jewish to follow him. Jesus was a Jew, after all. We heard that we'd need to follow all the Jewish laws about what to eat and how to wash, and that our husbands and sons would have to be circumcised.

But then the message began leaking out that Jesus would accept us just as we are—no changing of customs or adopting new rituals. And thank God, because the men weren't exactly jumping on the circumcision bandwagon.

Though even now that we know Jesus accepts us the way we are, we wonder if the Jewish Christians will ever really accept us as part of their faith family. To be accepted by Jesus is one thing, but to be welcomed by his followers is quite another.

The reading of the letter continues, and we hear these words: "But now in Christ Jesus you who once were far away have been brought near by the blood of Christ. For he himself is our peace" (Ephesians 2:13–14).

At those words—"he himself is our peace"—everyone gasps. People jump up from where they've been sitting to close the shutters that were open to the busy street and check the doors to make sure no one outside had been leaning in to spy on our meeting. We all glance around at each other's faces nervously for a moment, wondering if there could be a spy among us. For if anyone heard those words— "he himself is our peace"—we would certainly be dragged in for questioning, probably flogged, and then maybe arrested and imprisoned.

We've been under the iron rule of Rome for long enough to know what will stir up their wrath, so this phrase both thrills us with hope and chills us with the fear of certain persecution. On feast and festival days in Rome, especially on the birthday of the emperor, who was proclaimed to be a god, heralds would ride through the town shouting the emperor's accomplishments and celebrating his greatness. And one of the most repeated lines we'd hear every year would be this: "He is our peace. The emperor brings peace." The letter we are reading borrows those lines and replaces the emperor with Jesus, saying that peace is to be found only in him.

The Roman brand of peace, of course, is chaos incarnate, squashing with violence and dominance anyone who dares to defy the ruling powers. Anyone who risks challenging the emperor is simply silenced with force or, when necessary, with death. That's the kind of peace they proclaim.

The empire stops chaos with chaos and calls it peace— Pax Romana. But their brand of peace threatens, with swords and armor and prison cells at the waiting.

And here we are, daring to read aloud that true peace has come at last in the person of a man who was crucified by the Roman Empire. It's shocking to hear, but deep down we know these words are true. They are truer than any words we've ever heard the empire declare.

We've been a people defined by what we are not. We are not falling in line in submission to the hostile character of Rome outside the church. We dip our toe into the water of disobedience, but we know better than to openly defy them. But we are also not insiders to the Jewish Christians, the ones who began this movement we know as the church. We haven't bowed to their expectations that we become Jewish or adopt their practices and rules. The letter we're hearing seems to know both of these things about us, calling on the two groups (Gentiles and Jews) within the faith to merge into one:

> For [Christ] himself is our peace, who has made the two groups one and has destroyed the barrier, the dividing wall of hostility, by setting aside in his flesh the law with its commands and regulations. His purpose was to create in himself one new humanity out of the two, thus making peace, and in one body to reconcile both of them to God through the cross, by which he put to death their hostility. He came and preached peace to you who were far away and peace to those who were near. For through him we both have access to the Father by one Spirit.
>
> *Ephesians 2:14–18*

This letter seems to speak to exactly where we sit, squeezed between Roman oppression on the outside and Jewish expectation on the inside. And the most amazing thing is that the writer of this letter—a man named Paul—is himself locked in a Roman prison at this very moment. They've locked up his body, but it just makes his message travel faster, his words pouring out to us and to other churches like ours that are filling up with more and more and more people hungry for news of Jesus.

When we hear Paul's words read, we feel that someone caught behind prison walls finally understands the walls we face. Rome is good at building empires, building walls, building prisons for the people who disagree. The Jewish Christians we long to join are good at building walls of rules and systems and ways to climb to God we will never reach.

Conquering the tyranny of the human heart, with all the walls we build up against each other, even those walls inside a faith—that would take a true miracle.

Imagine you were in church in Ephesus the first day this letter was read.

Hearing for the first time the idea that you could belong—truly belong to God and to other Christians and to an empire that would outlast Rome. Imagine getting news that you were no longer second-class citizens. That would surely be a day you would never forget.

Jump Forward

Now, imagine you're in church.

A different church in a different time—the twenty-first century.

This church looks a lot different from the last one you imagined. It's a traditional church building located in the traditional-looking suburbs in a neighborhood filled with ranch-style homes and dotted with grocery stores and family-style restaurants.

The church is the largest in the area, a landmark that people use to point out directions. It's a beautiful building—a sanctuary filled with stained glass, a huge fellowship hall for meals. The most beautiful room in the place is the church parlor, with its beautiful cream-colored carpet, which is used mostly by the women's club and for special events, but has strict rules forbidding any children's events or the consumption of red punch.

In the last year we've added on to our beautiful landmark building a big gymnasium with a basketball court and a weight room with showers. We went into a great deal of debt to build the addition and are counting on it to attract new people into the church. Mostly when we talk about attracting new people, we're talking about the right kind of people with the right kind of money to pay off the debt we incurred to build the building.

Every Friday, the Rotary Club meets in the fellowship hall at the middle of the church, with the mayor, police chief, and all kinds of local bigwigs milling around and eating homemade chicken fried steak and strawberry shortcake. Those gatherings make us another kind of landmark in the community, known and recognized as a place where people come to see and be seen.

But the community itself has changed a lot since the church was built a few decades ago. Apartment complexes have popped up on the corners opposite the church, and taquerias and Mexican-style bakers have begun to crowd out some of the family-style restaurants. Most of the newer residents moving into our neighborhood speak Spanish as their first and sometimes as their only language. To those who have lived here for decades, all the change feels a lot like chaos.

This church is generous to their neighbors, so they put on lots of events for the community. There's a huge Easter egg hunt and a summer carnival and a big Halloween event known as trunk-or-treat, where church members park their cars in the parking lot and hand out candy to neighborhood kids. The church is generous toward the community, but there's a lot of us doing the giving to a lot of them—and not a lot of meeting of the two. The whole neighborhood turns out for the Saturday night carnivals, but none of them come back for a worship service on Sunday mornings.

When nearby residents do show up, it's not on Sunday but during the week. They come to the church office and ask for help. Their lights are about to be turned off. They're out of formula. Their husband has left them. They're about to be evicted. We're a big church with a lot of resources—can't we help?

So many people come every day that the church secretary can't get her work done, so we open up an assistance office, and two volunteers sit at a desk handing out vouchers for the electric company, gift cards to Walmart, and directions to the local food bank. The line stretches down the hall most days and during the holidays out the door and around the block.

So imagine you're in church, and one day you're walking down the hall to your office. (Did I forget to mention that you work at this church?) Every day you walk down the hall and step around people who are in line for assistance in order to get to your office where you get ministry done. They are in your way on your way to do ministry, so you politely say, "Excuse me," and hurry to answer phone calls and emails and plan Sunday worship services.

Only that day as you're stepping around people in the

hallway, something catches your eye. It's the sweetest baby face looking up at you, a face framed with curls and smeared with chocolate. He's dressed in only a soggy diaper and looks like he hasn't had a bath in a while, but when he looks up at you and sees you looking down at him, he grins, and it's love at first sight for you both.

His name is Baby Joey. That's what they call him, because it's his daddy's name too. His parents, Renee and Joe, are sitting beside him on the floor of the church hallway, filling out church forms so they can get assistance. And for some reason, for the first time in all the days you've walked down the hall past all those people, you sit down on the floor and talk to them.

They're both unemployed. They've run out of formula and diapers for the baby, and when you ask them where they live, they don't really want to tell you. They hem and haw and avoid the question until finally they tell you the thing they don't want to admit: this is their only address. They are sleeping in their car in the big parking lot behind the church at night and then driving around during the day and taking turns with the baby while they look for jobs.

As you walk with them down the hall to a closet where you know extra diapers and formula are stored, it occurs to you that today is Wednesday, and this church is in the habit of eating together every Wednesday night. Christians still eat together as often as possible. Some things haven't changed since the first century. Instead of just sending them out the door with the groceries and gift cards you know the assistance office will give them, you ask if they could join you for dinner. You are serious but doubtful they'll take you up on it. Then that night you are surprised when they actually show up.

You're surprised, but ready, since you've spent the afternoon on the phone, first asking if you could allow them access to the fancy new showers and dressing rooms in the church's gym. The church's trustees nixed that one fast but then surprised you by telling you about a member who is part owner of a local hotel. That phone call went even better, with the member offering a room until they could get more permanent lodging. (A homeless ten-month-old tends to get people to listen.) Other leaders started chipping in gift cards for groceries, and while you were prepared to go out in the parking lot to look for them, they walk into dinner that night beaming like honored guests.

They've put a fresh onesie on little Joey, and he reaches out for you like you're old friends. You sit with them at dinner and introduce them around, and people welcome them and listen to parts of their story. And that's where you begin to learn for the first time about how desperately chaotic life can be when you are poor. They've found jobs and lost jobs. Rented apartments and lost apartments. They've lived next to crack houses and barely dodged a drive-by. Once, Renee found a job that would pay more than what they needed to live week to week, and it looked like they might get to save a little until they'd have enough to live in another part of town. When her employer found out she was pregnant, they fired her that week. Joe has been hospitalized off and on with kidney issues, but they have no way to pay the medical bills. You ask about family—he has none and hers is so abusive she fled before she was eighteen and vowed never to go back.

Think of all the safeguards you've had in your life, all the privileges that mean there are a hundred steps between you and living in your car. They have none of them. You had no idea that people lived in the expectation that the floor can fall out from under them at any moment. You had no idea they were right.

You tell them about the hotel room and introduce them to the person who will drive over with them and help them get settled. They are thankful to the point of tears. When they leave that night, Baby Joey already asleep on his dad's shoulder, you wonder if that's the last you'll see of them.

But the next Wednesday night, they're back! You hear about their job-hunting adventures and Baby Joey's ear infection and navigating the lines at the free clinic. Weeks pass, and they come back Wednesday after Wednesday. You visit them at the charity hospital when big Joe has another kidney attack and then you visit him when he lands in the local jail—a misunderstanding, they assure you. They show up at your office unannounced in between Wednesdays most weeks in one crisis or another, but they come less and less for handouts and more because you listen. And because you love their baby.

And when they're on their feet enough to scrape together the deposit for an apartment, they choose one right across the street. Now when you look out the window at the ugly apartment complexes that church members say are ruining the neighborhood, you see them with different eyes.

You learn the apartment has no furniture. They're sleeping on the floor. So on Christmas morning, you show up at the apartment complex with a group of people from the church, the beds of their pickup trucks loaded down. Someone has a couch they don't need, another person a bed, and someone's baby has outgrown their crib. There are new sheets and towels and Christmas groceries.

You and the others sing carols under their window until they open up and see you there with a house full of furniture and Christmas breakfast just for them. They look at it like they're not quite sure it's real.

Then one Sunday morning, you're in your pastoral robes bookmarking the day's passage in your Bible when you look out over the church sanctuary as the worship service starts and realize, to your shock, they've come to church. They've been here on Wednesdays a lot. Tuesdays and Thursdays and Mondays too. But never on Sunday.

They're dressed in jeans and work boots, and Baby Joey is squirming and crying in just his diaper. You hold your breath when the people around them turn to look. You pray the church ladies will be kind, that no one will hiss that they should put that baby in the nursery. They don't know what a church nursery is or that they should take a crying baby out of the worship space. They don't know when to sit or stand, and you see someone hand them a hymnal opened to the right page. You relax a little. It's not really Renee's and Joe's behavior you were worried about, or even the baby's. You wondered if this nice church that helps so many people outside would welcome them inside.

They see a baptism that morning and ask how much money it takes to pay to get little Joey baptized. When you tell them baptisms are free, they're excited, but then they tell you a secret. They never had a chance to get married. Could you do a wedding first?

So one Friday, you help Renee get ready for her wedding in the sacred church parlor, the precious room reserved for the women's teas. And she looks beautiful in a secondhand dress. And after you pronounce them husband and wife in the sanctuary, the church women throw them a reception in the fellowship hall, where Baby Joey is practicing walking and falling down and getting up again, all with a fistful of wedding cake in his hand.

Imagine you're in church.

Imagine you're in church one Sunday, and someone stands up to read a letter. It's that same letter read by the little house church in Asia Minor almost two thousand years before in AD 60. The letter written by the man in chains is still circulating, still speaking to those who long to hear the story of the crucified God. Still urging that the walls humans build to make them feel safer from humans on the other side be brought down:

> He came and preached peace to you who were far away and peace to those who were near. For through him we both have access to the Father by one Spirit.
>
> Consequently, you are no longer foreigners and strangers, but fellow citizens with God's people and also members of his household, built on the foundation of the apostles and prophets, with Christ Jesus himself as the chief cornerstone.
>
> *Ephesians 2:17–20*

Imagine that as you hear someone read these words to the comfortable congregation, you look out and see a baby's familiar curls bobbing in his mother's arms in the back row, and you close your eyes as you hear, "You are no longer foreigners. No longer strangers. You are fellow citizens now. Members of the household of God."

And you pray, *Please, Jesus. Let it be true. Let it be true. Let these words come true here in this church.*

They come back again and again. They fight, they separate, they get back together. Joe goes back to jail. He gets out. Neither of them can keep a job for more than a couple months. They get so behind on rent that they leave their apartment in the middle of the night and lose all the furniture and most of their belongings. They get a new apartment. It all starts over again.

And then one day, they don't come back. And you never see them again. And you always wonder about them. Little Joey would be a teen now, and even if he doesn't remember any of it, you hope that somehow something lasting was built for him in the year you saw him turn one.

Well-Organized Religion

Imagine you're in church.

What do you see? These days, it could resemble a suburban sanctuary or first-century house church, cathedral, or storefront—or something in between. But imagining church may not mean imagining a building. What is it then? A group? A club? An institution?

It seems a fashion of our age to complain about institutions. Where once we trusted lives, families, and careers to them, we now find that institutions are to blame for many of our problems. Much has been said and written about the flaws of "organized religion," and many people bear its scars.

But well-organized religion can be a perfect counter to organized chaos. If that sounds like an oxymoron, it's no surprise, since we tend to think of chaos, by definition, as disorganized. But imagine a hurricane sweeping slowly across open water as it picks up speed inside its circular maelstrom. Meteorologists talk about the power of hurricanes by naming how "organized" they become, the choreographed dance of deadly winds moving in tighter and tighter circles. A highly organized storm can hit a coastline and knock flat everything in its path.

If winds can be organized into systems, so too can evil. The confession that "we live in a sinful world" doesn't only mean individuals sin against other individuals, but it also means the swirling winds of our age are organized into systems that work to keep those in low positions low, those who have privilege high, those who are insiders in, and those who are marginalized out.

Almost every church has walls; walls that keep us together and safe and dry while we worship and serve, but there are the other kinds of walls too—walls that keep some in and some out. Drawing lines that determine who belongs and who doesn't keeps us feeling comfortable and safe in a different way.

In just the next few lines of that same letter, read to

first-century and twenty-first-century Christians alike, we read about how God wants church walls to work. They are designed to be "built on the foundation of the apostles and prophets, with Christ Jesus himself as the chief cornerstone. In him the whole building is joined together and rises to become a holy temple in the Lord. And in him you too are being built together to become a dwelling in which God lives by his Spirit" (Ephesians 2:20–22). A cornerstone is the first stone laid, the stone that shapes the rest of the work. If the cornerstone is true to square, the building will be too. If the cornerstone is off, the rest will be unstable. The thing about a cornerstone is that it joins walls together, taking lines that might never converge and creating between them a corner.

To imagine a church is to imagine a system, a place where people who have been slammed by the winds of institutional chaos find peace. Those who would never meet in boardrooms or soup lines sit together in worship and eat together in fellowship. These walls only meet in Christ. And when one meets another, as Jesus said, "On this rock I will build my church, and the gates of hell shall not prevail against it" (Matthew 16:18 ESV).

Imagine you're in church. Imagine what God could build. Maybe it's time to imagine again.

CONCLUSION
Travelers

Years before I embarked on the overwhelming journey to parenthood, I took baby steps into ministry in a small, rural church. Someone had the bright idea of putting me in charge of the teens, even though I was only a few years older than the high school seniors in the group. My own life's chaos was barely under control, so I wasn't quite sure how I was going to whip anyone else's chaos into shape, which is what I think the teens' parents expected me to do.

The church was in a tiny town down a country road from where I grew up. It was an interesting mix of family farms and trailer parks, and in the middle of it all, a brand-new gated community had just popped up. It had a manicured golf course at the center and new McMansions popping up around it every week. I was never sure what the gates were meant to keep out. The neighbor's cows?

Because the town was so small and there wasn't much else going on, I convinced seven high school students to spend every Tuesday night for an entire school year reading the Bible together. A Bible study sounded like the right answer to their boredom and my lack of ideas about what in the world I was doing. I thought it might give all of us some focus, or at least get the parents off my back.

And we needed some kind of focus, because I was pretty sure most of the teens were not there because I convinced them to come. Most of them weren't even there because they wanted to study the Bible.

At least two of the boys were there because they had a crush on the same girl. A small flock of boys seemed to follow her like a cloud wherever she went, and so when she signed up, there was an immediate spike in interest in Bible study by participants of the male persuasion.

One girl, Audrey, was there just to get away from how bad things were at home. Chaos buzzed around her family in such an electric way that I could feel it just beneath the surface as I talked to her parents after church while she stood by, silently staring at her shoes.

Another girl, Lizzie, had declared she didn't believe in all that "Christian stuff" anymore, but her parents were forcing her to attend. They believed a year studying the Bible with me was the last hope to resurrect their daughter's faith. No pressure or anything.

Then there was Justin. He was easily the quietest kid in the group. He talked more during the car trip to church when I went to pick him up for Bible study each week than he did in the entire two hours we were with the class. Justin lived on a long gravel road that backed up to the gated community. You could see the McMansions over the backs of their fences, but in front of them was a road lined with double-wide trailers whose front yards were littered with the rusting shells of old pickup trucks. The farther you drove down that gravel road, the more rundown the trailers became. And Justin lived at the very end at an address even the mail carrier tried to avoid.

I always prayed he'd be waiting on the front porch when I arrived each week to pick him up. If he wasn't, I'd have to turn the car off, get out, and walk up the path to the front steps. When I did, a pack of a dozen small dogs would appear out of nowhere, barking wildly and nipping at my ankles while I tried to ring the doorbell.

Justin and I had a lot of great talks on those drives down the gravel road on the way to church. We talked about things like this year's football team or his dream of getting an athletic scholarship and becoming the first person in his family to go to college. Sometimes he'd talk about harder things, like his mom who was tired from working several jobs or his stepdad's drinking.

On one of those drives, I noticed his legs were covered in insect bites that had been scratched raw, and he confided in me that things had gotten a little too crowded and loud in the trailer lately, and he had been sleeping in the wooden shed out back at night. He was doing his homework and reading for Bible study out there by flashlight, pretending he was camping. It was pretty okay, he told me, except there was no air conditioning and he was sharing space with the pack of dogs, and they had a bad case of fleas.

I know you're not supposed to have favorites in ministry, but Justin was mine. He seemed like a kid I could really make a difference with. The others had chaos in their lives, certainly, but there always seemed to be an adult behind the scenes somewhere helping them sort it out. I was pretty sure they'd all be okay eventually. But Justin—well, Justin needed me. And I liked being needed. I thought I might be the only grown-up showing up and paying attention to Justin, and as a newly minted adult myself, it made me feel more like a grown-up to think I could make a difference in his life.

If Justin was the quietest kid in the group, then Lee made up for him several times over. Lee was a late addition to the group. The eighth one to sign up.

I had announced this was going to be a senior high Bible study. High school kids only. I didn't think the announcement was necessary, because no junior high kid I had ever met would want to spend every Tuesday night for a year reading the Bible anyway.

But one did—little redheaded Lee, who ran up to me after our youth meeting one week and told me in his high, squeaky voice that he wanted to join the Bible study. He was years younger and light-years less mature than the other kids joining the study. I told him no, that this was for the older kids in our youth group. And I thought (naively) that if you told a kid no, that was the end of it.

The next week, Lee asked me again. And he asked again the next. And the next. I told him no every week. I told him he'd have to wait until he was in high school to study the Bible. I stood my ground: "Stop asking!" I said. "You're too young!" And he finally gave up. Or so I thought. Then one week he came up to me with a question. "Miss Jessica," he said, "how does that beast in Revelation wear ten crowns if it only has seven heads?"

That got my attention. I asked him, "How do you know about that beast in Revelation?"

Lee said, "Well, I've been reading Revelation every night before I go to bed. I love the gory battles and all the monsters and stuff. And I've probably read it ten times now, but I just can't figure that beast out!"

And he opened his notebook and showed me drawing after drawing detailing all the beasts and battles and gore of Revelation. They were actually pretty good.

And that was it. Any kid who was reading the book of Revelation as light bedtime reading was welcome to join a Bible study. Even if he was the youngest by far. It turned out that at thirteen years old, he was more dedicated and disciplined than most of the seniors in high school. Lee loved chaos. Battles. Blood. His favorite pastime was annoying the older boys in the group, but he kept us all awake and kept me on my toes.

No Other Story

That first Tuesday night, we sat around a table in the church library—those who were eager to be there, those who were reluctant, and those who were trying to impress a girl. And we started by reading together out loud, "In the beginning God created the heavens and the earth. Now the earth was formless and empty, and darkness was over the surface of the deep, and the Spirit of God was hovering over the waters."

We learned right away that the Bible was a messy book. God seemed to have his work cut out for him. It was right there on page 1. Things could get pretty dark sometimes. Maybe that's why God's first words were, "Let there be light."

What I couldn't have known that first Tuesday night was how desperately every kid around that table needed to hear those words. Over the course of that year, we would glimpse just how chaotic, empty, and dark each of the lives gathered there could be at times, and how desperately we each needed God to work on us. That night, I remember wishing I could see God hovering in that room in the same way he hovered over those chaotic waters—with the protective gentleness of a mother bird willing our chaotic cracks into a hatching of order and light.

We also learned that first night that God started the whole world in a garden. I could tell that kind of appealed to the kids who lived in the country or on a farm. They knew from experience that the consequences of someone's actions can affect everyone around them. If you neglected your chores and responsibilities, your whole livelihood and even the lives of your animals were at stake. We learned that when Adam and Eve messed up—really, every time humans messed up—the consequences spread. Chaos and darkness and emptiness crept back in. But that every time that happened, God stepped in too with light, order, and hope.

It seemed like a lot of the Old Testament was about God's people messing up and needing his help. Sometimes it seemed like the ones who showed up at Bible study were getting something out of it, maybe even on the verge of enjoying it. But a lot of the time they goofed off or didn't do their reading for that week—or didn't show up at all.

Somewhere in the middle of the Old Testament, things started to drag a little. (If I'm honest, it wasn't even in the middle. It was definitely more toward the beginning that the grumbling started.) That happens sometimes when you read the Bible from beginning to end. You get slowed down by all those parts near the beginning—genealogies and laws and measurements of every single little part of the temple. Lee kept complaining that this part was nothing like Revelation, that there were no cool dragons or beasts. Like a little kid in the back seat during a long road trip, he kept asking when we were going to get to the good stuff.

I remember one Tuesday night in particular, we were in the middle of an especially repetitive part of the book of Judges when Lee, our little redheaded, squeaky-voiced, Revelation-reading junior high pip-squeak piped up all of a sudden. "Wait a minute, wait a minute," he said. "Didn't we just read this?"

"Read what?" I asked.

"Well," he said, "that phrase, for starters—'The Israelites did evil in the eyes of the LORD.' It said it on the last page—and the page before that. And here it is again: 'Again the Israelites did evil in the eyes of the LORD.'" He sighed deeply. "In the last chapter, the people did evil in the eyes of the Lord, and bad things happened to them. They got attacked and beat up and made slaves, so they needed God's help. And they cried out to him, and he came to rescue them, and then things were great! But they keep taking their eyes off God and trying to do it themselves. They keep screwing up whenever they rely on themselves instead of God, and then it says it *again*! 'Again the Israelites did evil in the eyes of the LORD.' Then bad things start happening, and they need God's help . . . And it all starts all over again!"

His voice was getting higher and squeakier. "I'm getting tired of this!" he said. "Isn't there *some other story*?"

We all had a good laugh for a minute at how red in the face our little group mascot had gotten. But then there was one of those rare moments where everything got quiet, where someone has said something profound without really meaning to, and everyone is thinking the exact same thing. That really, there is no other story.

That's it. That's the story. God's people are in trouble; they need him; and he always comes through, always delivers them, rescues them. He brings them out of Egypt, returns them from exile, rescues them from oppressors or famine or destruction. He helps them survive a tough math test or calms them while their parents are screaming in the next room or makes sure there's someone they can talk to when things are at their roughest. And they are grateful . . . for a while. But then they get complacent. They think they can do things their own way—that they don't need God—and that always leads to trouble. And it begins all over again.

Chaos wasn't just an event; it was a cycle. We had all seen it. It wasn't just the story of some old book we were reading together; it was each of our own stories as well.

When Sheep Wander Off

It was almost spring before we finally turned the pages to the New Testament. Jesus was born around Valentine's Day. It seemed odd to read the Christmas story on the wrong holiday, but in a way, entering into it without the craziness of Christmas season helped Jesus' birth seem like a brand-new story. Maybe for the first time we didn't just breeze past it on our way to the Christmas parties and gifts.

We noticed that, as Jesus grew up, everything he touched started to look a lot like the garden at the beginning of the story. Everywhere he went, chaos parted like the waters of the Red Sea. Wherever he found sickness, emptiness, sin, and death, he stopped it and brought life instead.

Jesus, we decided, was taking on God's job description from back in the beginning. He was all about bringing light to darkness, order to chaos, fullness to emptiness.

It was around that time that Lizzie, whose parents had forced her to come, confided in me that she just might believe in God after all. And I was feeling pretty good about myself. Like I wasn't just wasting my time every Tuesday night in this little church library. Like maybe I was supposed to be teaching people the Bible after all. Maybe I was actually good at this ministry thing.

And then one Tuesday afternoon when I drove down the long gravel road to pick up Justin, my favorite, from the last trailer in the long line of trailers, he wasn't on the porch. I braved the pack of ankle-nipping, flea-bitten dogs to climb the steps of the front porch and ring the doorbell, and his mother's face appeared behind the screen door and told me he wasn't there. That he wasn't coming. That Justin was in jail.

She said it so matter-of-factly that it was like he had gone out for a walk. He was seventeen.

Justin had spent the weekend with some friends his mom called "a bad influence." He was one of those kids who was a follower. He did great at football practice following the plays or at church following the crowd, but that particular weekend, he had followed the wrong friends with the wrong idea.

They had decided what would go well with their late-night shenanigans was some beer, so they had taken a couple of four-wheelers and ridden down to a convenience store they knew was closed, thrown a brick in a window, climbed in, and stolen cases of beer. There was just one flaw in their little plan. When they drove away through the muddy field, their four-wheelers left tracks, leading the police straight back to the house where they were staying, where they were soon all arrested.

Justin was seventeen, but they decided to charge him as an adult. And while all the other kids' parents had bailed them out, he was the last one still sitting in jail. None of his family showed up. In a small town, word travels fast. I knew some parents were saying he shouldn't be allowed to come to the church's youth group anymore, that this one bad kid was going to be a bad influence on their good kids.

I found myself doing something I had no idea could be part of youth ministry. Instead of driving to Justin's football games or driving to pick him up for church, I was driving to visit him in the county jail. Those conversations as I faced Justin on the other side of the glass were some of the deepest conversations about Jesus I've ever had with any person, much less between a twenty-two-year-old and a seventeen-year-old in the county jail. They let us bring him a Bible, and he read it like his life depended on it, not just like it was for Bible study class. He told me that God had really transformed him while he was sitting in jail, and that he felt called to tell people about Jesus when he got out, to help other people like him.

When his hearing came, the judge decided since it was his first offense, he could release him with probation to the pastor and to me. His family never did show up. As we drove back to town, he said he didn't want to go home. It was Tuesday, and he wanted to go to Bible study.

That night when we opened the book of Matthew, Jesus was telling a story. One of the girls read it aloud: "If a man owns a hundred sheep, and one of them wanders away, will he not leave the ninety-nine on the hills and go to look for the one that wandered off? And if he finds it, truly I tell you, he is happier about that one sheep than about the ninety-nine that did not wander off" (Matthew 18:12–13).

I looked up across the table just as Justin caught my eye and mouthed, "Thank you."

Over the next few weeks, his life seemed totally transformed. Justin had always been known as a follower, but now it seemed like he was leading the pack in following Jesus. Even the grown-ups were amazed.

On youth Sunday he stood in the pulpit of that church and gave his testimony of transformation, and the congregation cried and applauded, and then Justin called me up to the front and pulled a bouquet of flowers out of the pulpit and handed them to me and told the whole church that it was all because of me that his life had changed. He gave me a hug, and everyone clapped and sang "Amazing Grace." And then we went and ate fried chicken.

I thought, *If this is ministry, I think I can do this. I've got this thing down. I saved a kid.* I felt like I was ready to take on the world. And within two weeks, Justin was back in jail.

He had gone for his probation meeting and failed the drug test, having smoked pot with the same friends with the four-wheelers the night before. He was a great follower, this kid. It's just that he hadn't figured out who to follow yet.

That week, I spiraled into the deepest hole I had ever been in. I crawled under the covers in my room, where I was living at home with my mom, and tried to think of ways I could never come out again. Maybe I could quit my job. Or my life. Or just run away and go to grad school.

I had failed. I couldn't face the church or the youth or their parents again. I had lost the one kid who was most important to save. Every sentence of my pity party began with "I."

And I don't remember how long I sat there feeling sorry for myself in the tiny world I had built that revolved around me, but eventually I heard God's voice. And what God said to me wasn't exactly comforting: *If you want the credit,* he said, *you're going to have to take the blame too. If it's you who saves these kids, it's going to be you who loses them. If you let them put you on a pedestal, the fall from grace is going to be just as devastating as the view. If you are in this business for what the people say when they praise you, you're going to have to own the criticism too.*

God's voice can be brutally honest sometimes.

So I confessed what I already knew: that there was nothing in me that could save anyone, not even myself. That I was going to have to depend on God for all of it, because I really had no idea what I was doing. Twenty years of life and ministry later, that fact really hasn't changed.

I crawled out of my hole and went back to work. And to Tuesday night Bible study, but I was different. I don't think I've ever been the same, really. Chaos was more real than it had ever been, and so was my awareness that I'd be stupid to try to take it on myself.

Full Circle

At the end of April, we finally got to the book of Revelation. We let little redheaded Lee read his favorite parts aloud. He had drawn pictures of the beasts and dragons and the lion and lamb and taped them up around the Sunday school classroom in celebration of our last Tuesday night together.

When I looked around that table, I could see a difference in the face of every one of those teens from where we had started on the first Tuesday night. Chaos was still real, still looming in some way for each of them, but so was the awareness of the God who spoke chaos into order. Now we knew where he was in the chaos, and we knew we could trust him with it.

Justin wasn't there that night. He didn't come back to

youth group again. He did get in touch with me on Facebook a few years ago to show me pictures of his kids and tell me about his construction job and his church. And to talk about what had happened all those years ago and how it had changed both of us.

But that night, we left his chair empty at the table as we finished our yearlong study together. And as Lee was reading aloud in his squeaky voice, in characteristic Lee fashion, he got mad at the Bible. He got mad reading Scripture a lot. That night, he was mad that the dragons and beasts and horror and gore had all ended. He had been so excited to get there, but now the chaos had been swallowed up, and order, fullness, and light had been restored. "I thought we were just getting to the good part," Lee complained, "but this looks just like the boring, old, first story again. Gardens and trees and rivers. Same old story all over again." Sure enough, Lee's eye for scriptural interpretation was sound, even if his attitude was a little off.

God had somehow brought us full circle back to the start. "I am making everything new!" it says in Revelation 21:5—and by new it means the very newness of Eden dawning again. The last page of the Bible looks remarkably like the first.

Fellow Travelers

Thinking about our little band of travelers who met together each Tuesday night reminded me of a magazine article I had spotted about how NASA was preparing to honor the thirtieth anniversary of the Apollo 8 mission in December 1968. Our little town was close enough to Houston that several of our church members worked in industries that supported NASA, and for those communities, the Apollo missions were still remembered as the golden age. The year Apollo 8 launched, however, was known more for its age of chaos.

The Vietnam War was wreaking havoc; the resulting protests sharply divided American culture. The assassinations of Dr. Martin Luther King Jr. and Robert Kennedy, the brother of the recently assassinated president John F. Kennedy, rocked any sense of stability and predictability of life. These events and others unframed life as the world once knew it.

In the midst of this world that was coming unglued, the Apollo 8 mission succeeded in putting three astronauts in space to orbit the moon, a precursor to the Apollo 11 mission just six months later that would land the first human on the surface of the moon in 1969.

The pictures those first orbiting astronauts on Apollo 8 sent back—the first taken of earth from a distance—projected an image of creation that restored some sense of perspective and serenity in a deeply troubled time. The singular blue marble floating in space seemed, from a distance, a miracle, the chaos of riots and assassinations and wars on its surface placed into tiny perspective.

On Christmas Eve 1968, the crew offered a live television broadcast from lunar orbit. Command module pilot Jim Lovell said, "The vast loneliness is awe-inspiring and it makes you realize just what you have back there on Earth."[19]

Then the crew offered earth an extraordinary gift. NASA permitted the three astronauts to choose whatever Christmas message they wanted to offer the people of their home planet. Today it's hard to picture three men being given such latitude in what a global broadcast would contain, but here is what they chose to say with words that would be widely heard by many, many households back on their home. This is a script of what they spoke over our planet as they projected never-before-seen pictures of creation, zoomed out to a distance that offered a needed perspective of peace amid chaos.

William Anders:

For all the people on Earth the crew of Apollo 8 has a message we would like to send you:

"In the beginning God created the heaven and the earth.

"And the earth was without form, and void; and darkness was upon the face of the deep.

"And the Spirit of God moved upon the face of the waters. And God said, Let there be light: and there was light.

"And God saw the light, that it was good: and God divided the light from the darkness."

Jim Lovell:

"And God called the light Day, and the darkness he called Night. And the evening and the morning were the first day.

"And God said, Let there be a firmament in the midst of the waters, and let it divide the waters from the waters.

"And God made the firmament, and divided the waters which were under the firmament from the waters which were above the firmament: and it was so.

"And God called the firmament Heaven. And the evening and the morning were the second day."

Frank Borman:

"And God said, Let the waters under the heavens be gathered together unto one place, and let the dry land appear: and it was so.

"And God called the dry land Earth; and the gathering together of the waters called he Seas: and God saw that it was good."

Borman then added, "And from the crew of Apollo 8, we close with good night, good luck, a Merry Christmas, and God bless all of you—all of you on the good Earth."[20]

The good earth. Even from far away, this crew could see what those on the ground could not. Taking a step back to view its planetary situation from a perspective far away in space, humanity had a glimpse of order among chaos, light in darkness, fullness in emptiness. They had a chance to view these as God's ongoing method of grace. And as God had once done in the beginning, the astronauts named creation "good."

The article about the Apollo 8 Christmas message reminded me that before my time, before the time of the teens who sat around a table with me each Tuesday night, that mission gave a dramatically countercultural view of creation, changing the perspective and memory of

1968 forever. Before the Apollo 8 mission launched, *Time* magazine had planned on naming "The Dissenter" as their "Person of the Year" that year. But after this extraordinary event, it gave the title to the crew of Apollo 8. Cosmic travelers journeying together in orbit around a place they called home had found peace in the midst of chaos through an ancient text. They offered that unique vision to those back home who were struggling to live in the turmoil close-up. It felt not unlike what we were doing on Tuesday nights in the church library, over teenage crushes and gossip and much more life-shaping events of arrest and probation and bail. What were we doing there each week if not orbiting together and peering out closely over creation to find our place in God's story—the same old story of God converting chaos—and asking him, please, to do it again?

ACKNOWLEDGMENTS

In my office hangs a large mosaic—so heavy that it once fell off the wall and dislodged several pieces of the ceramic tiles that form the picture. I walked in after one weekend to find them scattered across the carpet. The picture itself is of overlapping swirls of different shades of blue. I like to think it looks like waves washing over each other at the shore. A chaotic but beautiful pattern of forces pushing and pulling, all made up of these little blue tiles that were broken in order to piece them together to make art. It occurs to me now that somehow the cover of this book resembles that image, and I'm not exactly sure how God arranged that.

I think of this book a bit like that mosaic. There were so many little pieces that had to come together, and many of those originated outside of myself in conversations, contributions, and relationships. Many of the people involved brought their own chaotic pieces to the table and offered them as stories, support, listening ears—and all of that put together made something new.

I'm grateful for all who had a hand in forming what I'd been calling "the chaos book" for the last several years. For those who reflected on different pieces of the book, including reading rough and raw material: Hunter Bethea, Guy Wimberly, Bethany Barker, and Jessica Avery. For sharing your story and your life: Sabrina Toney and others whose stories have become precious parts of the mosiac. And for Joe and Renee and Baby Joey, wherever you are today.

I'm thankful for professionals who knew how to offer guidance, coaching, and an editing hand: Ann Kroeker, who brought clarity as an incredible writing coach; Ryan Pazdur and Nancy Erickson at Zondervan and their incredible team; and J. D. Walt and the team at Seedbed. Thank you for seeing a need in this world for a book on chaos.

And for Jim, Drew, and Kate, who patiently permitted my long ramblings on the topic of chaos, searched out stories and details to share as their offerings for the book, and tolerated my receding often to the chair upstairs in our chaotically happy home to write—thank you for all the meals, snacks, and stuffed animals to serve as writing coaches and the ideas that always came with hugs generously shared. I'm thankful our life together has just the right touch of chaos most days to keep me on my toes.

NOTES

1. See Victor P. Hamilton, *The Book of Genesis: Chapters 1–17* (Grand Rapids: Eerdmans, 1990), 109, his translation.
2. See 2 Corinthians 5:17.
3. Carl Sagan, *Cosmos* (1980; repr., New York: Ballantine Books, 2013), 230.
4. G. K. Chesterton, *Orthodoxy*, vol. 1 in *The Collected Works of G. K. Chesterton: Heretics, Orthodoxy, The Blatchford Controversies*, ed. David Dooley (San Francisco: Ignatius, 1986), 300.
5. "Lucky Strike ad," *Popular Mechanics* 58, no. 6 (December 1932): back cover.
6. See Atul Gawande, *Being Mortal: Medicine and What Matters in the End* (New York: Metropolitan Books, 2014), 120.
7. Gawande, *Being Mortal*, 121.
8. *Jurassic Park*, directed by Steven Spielberg, starring Jeff Goldblum, Laura Dern, and Sam Neill (Los Angeles: Universal Pictures, 1993).
9. E. Stanley Jones, *Abundant Living* (1942; repr., Nashville: Abingdon, 2014), 16.
10. J. R. R. Tolkien, *The Return of the King*, vol. 3, *The Lord of the Rings* (1955; repr., New York: Ballantine Books, 1965), 246.
11. Isaac Watts, "Joy to the World." Public domain.

12. See Kathleen D. Vohs, Joseph P. Redden, and Ryan Rahinel, "Physical Order Produces Healthy Choices, Generosity, and Conventionality, Whereas Disorder Produces Creativity," *Psychological Science* 24, no. 9 (August 2013): 1860–67, https://doi.org/10.1177/0956797613480186.
13. See Andy Crouch, *Culture Making: Recovering Our Creative Calling* (Downers Grove, IL: InterVarsity, 2013), 22.
14. David Whyte, "Crossing the Unknown Sea," Gratefulness.org, https://gratefulness.org/resource/crossing-unknown-sea.
15. Carla D. Hayden, "Remembering John Lewis: The Power of 'Good Trouble,'" Library of Congress Blog, July 19, 2020, https://blogs.loc.gov/loc/2020/07/remembering-john-lewis -the-power-of-good-trouble.
16. See "Indian Ocean Tsunami of 2004," Britannica, www .britannica.com/event/Indian-Ocean-tsunami-of-2004
17. See "Mother in Photos Survived Tsunami," *BBC News*, January 2, 2005, http://news.bbc.co.uk/2/hi/europe/4141733 .stm; see also Alan Cowell, "From Image of Disaster to a Safe Homecoming," *New York Times*, January 3, 2005, www.nytimes.com/2005/01/03/world/worldspecial4/from -image-of-disaster-to-a-safe-homecoming.html.
18. Charles Wesley, "And Can It Be," in *Hymns and Sacred Poems*, ed. John and Charles Wesley (London: Strahan, 1739), 118, https://divinity.duke.edu/sites/divinity.duke .edu/files/documents/cswt/01_Hymns_and_Sacred_Poems _%281739%29_CW_Verse.pdf. Public domain.
19. Quoted in David Williams, "The Apollo 8 Christmas Eve Broadcast," NASA, December 24, 1968, last updated September 25, 2007, https://nssdc.gsfc.nasa.gov/planetary /lunar/apollo8_xmas.html.
20. Quoted in Williams, "Apollo 8 Christmas Eve Broadcast."